THE ADOPTION CONSTELLATION

*New Ways of Thinking About
and Practicing Adoption*

MICHAEL PHILLIP GRAND,

PhD, C.Psych

ISBN: 1452886903
ISBN-13: 9781452886909
Library of Congress Control Number: 2010910620

———————

To Jeanette who led me to the path, Kerry who encouraged me to walk with passion and Eileen who accompanied me each step of the way.

ACKNOWLEDGEMENTS

As soon will be obvious to the reader, one's narrative should be thought of as a co-construction in which many help to shape its themes. I would like to take this opportunity to personally thank and acknowledge those who played a part in the development of this book. Hy Day, my undergraduate supervisor recognized my academic propensities well before I had any glimmer that this would be my future direction. An early graduate student, Jeanette Cardiff, set my course as a researcher and clinician in adoption. Together we undertook one of the first studies on search and reunion. David Kirk, a seminal thinker in adoption, added wise lyrics to the melody of my narrative. Kerry Daly, a family sociologist, widened my thinking about systems as we served as the co-directors of the National Adoption Study of Canada. My political colleagues, Karen Lynn, Wendy Rowney, Nancy Kato, and Jim Kelly, by their example, directly contributed to the chapter on opening adoption records. A particular thanks must go to Monica Byrne. Together, our conference presentations across North America have served to sharpen my focus. Brenda Kenyon read an early draft of this work and encouraged me to persevere. Esther Budd kindly offered editorial assistance. Dan Perlman facilitated sabbaticals at the University of British Columbia. This book would not have been possible without the gift of reflective time. As "scholar in residence" at the Kinship Center of California, I have spent this past year observing, first hand, the emerging trends in adoptive practice. To all of the clinicians and staff and especially Sharon Rozsia, Carol Biddle, Carol Bishop, Allison Davis Maxon, Del Stewart, Ron Huxley, and Laura Ornelas, thank you for many wonderful conversations. Finally, I have been blessed with such a loving and supportive family: Eileen, Jacob, Dani, Avi and Ariella. Each of them, in their own special way, has taught me what it means to celebrate life. Thank you all.

CONTENTS

Acknowledgements   v

A Forethought   ix

   1. The Adoption Constellation   1

   2. The Primal Wound as Theory   7

   3. Adoption and Stigma   27

   4. A Narrative Understanding of Adoptive Experience   69

   5. Expanding the Choices   141

   6. Taking Our Principles to the Streets   161

A FORETHOUGHT

The beginning of a journey . . . In 1980 a graduate student came to me and said she wanted to do a Master's thesis on psychological and social factors that would predict whether adoptees would search for their birth parents. I rejected her request almost immediately. After all, what did I know about adoption? Months went by and almost weekly she came to my office to talk about the study she wished to undertake. In an attempt to keep up with the conversation, I began to read in the field. Of course, it was not long before I agreed to be her supervisor. A few weeks later, while reading her research proposal, I realized that my initial reluctance to supervise her work was a natural consequence of my personal history.

I was born the son of Allan and Mildred Grand, but a year after the death of my father, when I was seven, my mother remarried and I legally became Michael Sobol, the son of Stanley and Mildred Sobol. This was a classic 1950's step adoption. I was told not to mention my father to anyone. My paternal grandparents were banished from history. There was never to be any further contact with them. This stranger, my mother's second husband, was to be called "dad." Publically, it was a seamless transition from son of Allan to (adopted) son of Stanley. We never spoke of my father or how much I missed him. Tears dampened my pillow every night for over a year but no one knew. It was a grief that was never acknowledged, a pain that was never soothed. Interestingly, I did not think of myself as an adoptee. This is not surprising. Adoption was never discussed, so how could I accept "adoptee" as a personal moniker. At the age of seven, I had no understanding of what it meant to transfer parental rights and alter personal identity. As time went by, the emotional consequences of my adoption were all too real, but what they lacked was a language to describe these feelings and a cultural script that would allow me to ground myself in an identity that was consistent and true to my history. It was, thus, not surprising that when Jeanette Cardiff asked me to accompany her on a research journey to the heart of an adoptee's yearning, the search for birth parents, I failed to recognize that she was giving me an opportunity to come to terms with my own history. I was an adoptee, albeit, a step adoptee. I had the feelings for the role. I knew the melody. I just didn't know the words. Fortunately, with Jeanette's persistence, I came to realize that who I was as a person had been framed by my adoption. By launching me on a journey of personal reflection,[1] research and activism in the adoption community, she changed my life course and for this, I will always be grateful.

Adoption, today, is at a crossroads. Demographically, infant adoptions are no longer the norm (Sobol & Daly, 1992). Children who are older and who may display a range of challenging physical, cognitive and emotional characteristics make up the bulk of current adoptions. In addition, four other trends distinguish current adoption practice from the era when the placement of healthy infants was the norm.

Prospective adoptive parents, no longer satisfied to remain interminably on waiting lists for a domestic infant adoption, are turning overseas in search of a young child to adopt. In fact, it has been estimated that in the last decade there were three times as many infant overseas adoptions as there were infant domestic adoptions (Daly & Sobol, 1993).

---

1 Perhaps the most significant step in this journey occurred forty-nine years after our adoption. My brother and I and our four children all legally retook our family name, Grand.

The second trend reflects a major change in thinking in the field of adoption: Children in care, who were once thought not to be adoptable, are now being considered for adoption. No characteristic is assumed to make the child unadoptable. As the thinking goes, it is only a matter of finding the right family for any given child. Thus, we are seeing greater numbers of older children and those with multiple disabilities finding their way to adoptive homes.

The third major trend is that of openness. While often spoken of as a unitary concept, openness is best thought of as a dimension delineated at one end by the traditional closed adoption where no one has any contact or knowledge of the other parties to the adoption. At the other end of the spectrum, birth parents and the adoptive family are in personal contact throughout the course of the adoption without the auspices of a third party mediating their contact. Coupled with the demands of the activist community for access to closed adoption files, the past decade has been marked by a growing body of research evidence supporting more openness in adoption practice (Grotevant & McRoy, 1999).

The final trend represents the most dramatic turn in adoption practice, the possibility of embryo adoption. New reproductive technologies have resulted in a surplus of embryos beyond the needs of couples struggling to conceive a child. While religious sensibilities have stopped some from destroying these embryos, the question arises as to what to do with this genetic material. The answer that is gaining public support is that embryos should be made available for adoption in a fashion similar to the adoption of already-born children.

As these trends grow stronger we can no longer fall back on principles of adoption practice that reflect domestic infant placements from an earlier era of secrecy and closed files. Each of these trends presents new challenges to the definition of family, to the concept of the best interests of the child and to personal rights and responsibilities. They force us to ask serious questions about what adoption should look like in the future. Among the various paths of inquiry we may ask: Is adoption the best choice for building family relationships? Whose interests are taken into consideration when facilitating an adoption, particularly an open one? Whose voices have been silenced by adoption? Will an analysis of power relationships in adoption lead to a picture of adoption that is dramatically different from the one found in our prevailing cultural scripts? Why do adoptees, adoptive and birth parents and professionals have so much difficulty speaking to each other? What are the impediments to legislative change for opening sealed records?

My goal in this book is to challenge our conventional ways of thinking about adoption. We must look behind our current practices to discover the values that shape our actions. New metaphors will provide the adoption community with a wider choice of options for constructing family life. Today, it is estimated that thousands of children are awaiting placement into adoptive families. Most of these children are older and have special needs that were not as prevalent in past adoptions. We must ask ourselves whether the models of adoption that have been used for much of the last half century will be of much use as we consider the family constellations into which these children will be placed. And what of the concerns of the adoption activist community? We have heard cries to put a moratorium on adoption. Many declare that adoption is a painful process that, in the end, does not serve anyone's best interests. Sealed records are condemned for preventing access to one's history and the possibility of reconnection to birth family, which is viewed as a fundamental denial of human rights. All of these issues demand a response. To lay the groundwork for this task, we will begin with a consideration of the metaphors that have been used to describe the relationships between the constituent parties in adoption.

CHAPTER 1

THE ADOPTION CONSTELLATION

For much of the first half of the 20th century, the root metaphor for adoption was the nuclear family. Being adopted meant becoming the child of a heterosexual, married couple. The adoptive family was seen to be primarily dyadic in nature with the major focus on the adoptee and adoptive mother. Fathers were, for the most part, silent partners in these relationships. Birth parents were nowhere to be found. To highlight this fact, Frisk (1964) referred to birth families as "ghost" families. They were thought to lurk in the subconscious of the adoptee, a presence that could only disrupt the successful transformation of the adoptee into the "biological" child of the adoptive couple.

With the rise in interest in search and reunion and the appearance of birth parent activist organizations, a new metaphor, the adoption triad, became the metaphor of choice. The triad is usually displayed graphically as an equilateral triangle with the adoptee, birth parent (most likely, birth mother) and adoptive parents each occupying a corner of the triangle. This configuration was seen as an advancement in that it recognized that the birth parent was a real person with feelings and desires and was not simply an apparition in the mind of the adoptee. To this extent, the triad concept was a progressive move in thinking about the participants to the adoption. However, the choice of the equilateral triangle as the symbol of adoptive relationships failed to take into account the nature of these relationships. Firstly, being an equilateral triangle suggested that all three parties to the adoption held equal and equivalent power within their relationships. This clearly was not the case. The nature of parent-child relationships is rarely marked by equal power. Furthermore, birth parents, although recognized as participants in the adoption could hardly be seen as holding a position equivalent to that held by adoptive parents vis a vis the adoptive child. To carry this even further, given the closed nature of most adoptions, it is hard to imagine how they could even be presented as holding any significant position within this geometric display.

It is telling that the triad holds a much more prominent place in the literature of birth parent groups than it does for adoptive parent organizations who tend to focus on either their role as parents or their interactive relationships with their adoptive children. Thus, the triad has served as a metaphor for the birth parent community, particularly, to reflect their desire to be recognized as constituent members of the adoptive process. Birth parents do not wish to be written or displayed out of history. The triad, construed as an equilateral triangle, is a statement of the desire for a place in the adoptive process. It demands equal recognition of the role of the birth family. Given the static nature of the equilateral triangle, it says to the wider community, we are here and we won't go away. While these are laudatory goals, the triad and its current representation limit our thinking on adoption. It represents the hopes and aspirations of most birth parents and adoptees but does not reflect the position of those adoptive parents who have been more inclined to support closed adoptions. It also fails to represent the complexity and fluidity of adoptive and birth family relationships and so we must turn to an alternative configuration to meet this challenge.

Elsewhere (Grand, 2006), I have suggested that we need a systemic understanding that is broader in scope and more reflective of the changing shape of relationships in adoption. To assist in this task, I first proposed the concept of the adoption constellation (Sobol, 1994). This metaphor not only allows for the consideration of adoptees, birth parents and adoptive parents, but also incorporates birth and adoptive families, service providers, teachers, physicians, the courts, social service workers, legislators and the clergy. In fact, anyone whose life is entwined with adoption is a member of the constellation.

The adoption constellation is seen as changing shape across development as different relationships assume heightened or reduced emotional valence. In the beginning of the adoption, birth parents, adoptive parents, the child and the facilitator play the most prominent roles. Whether the adoption is an open one or not will alter the shape of the constellation. Closed adoptions diminish the luminance of the birth mother. Open adoptions may give her pride of place (Sobol, Daly & Kelloway, 2000). Private adoptions move the facilitator to the foreground (Daly & Sobol, 1994). During the early life of the adoption, extended family and friends play an important role in the constellation in terms of welcoming the new member and conferring social credibility on the nuclear family (Kirk, 1964). As the child enters the school system, teachers join the constellation. One need only think about how they manage the notion of family inclusion to observe their direct effect upon adoptive parent-child relationships. Friends of the adoptee also become salient at this point in that they may challenge the legitimacy of the family's definition. As the adoptee grows older, the peer group gains prominence, potentially pulling the adoptee in the direction of behaviors that will generate strong emotional responses on the part of the adoptive parents. Themes around risk taking, sexuality and fertility will have profound effects upon the shape of the adoptive family. If the adoptee or birth parent undertakes a search and if a reunion ensues, then elements of the constellation that have previously provided only background luminance, now become more salient. And if we leap ahead to the time when the adoptee becomes a parent, then this new addition will also help to form other emotional connections between members of the constellation.

Another advantage of using this systemic metaphor for adoptive relationships is that it allows for wider cultural forces such as societal attitudes and legislation to influence the shape of the constellation. In those jurisdictions where adoptions are traditionally closed and legislation limits the possibilities of birth family interacting with adoptive family, it would be expected that the distance between these two parts of the constellation would be great. However, this is not to say that the emotional gravitational pull between adoptee and birth family or adoptive parents and birth parents might not still be intense. In like manner, jurisdictions with open adoption legislation would be expected to have much less personal and emotional distance between constituent parties. Cultural attitudes about openness would have a parallel effect upon the placement of individuals in the constellation.

In summary, the metaphor of the adoption constellation allows for the changing shape and valence of relationships. It recognizes that with development, power relations take new forms. It encompasses the full range of individuals who have any connection to adoption. It might be pulled in the direction of the black holes of silence, restricted communication and closed records. It is also able to incorporate the changing shape of adoptive relationships marked by open adoption, single parent adoption and same-sex couple adoption. This metaphor allows for the recognition that various elements in the constellation play differing roles over time. Finally, by utilizing this concept, we are able to take into consideration the dynamic interactive influences that occur between the various elements of the constellation, thus, yielding a more systemic view. As such, each element in the constellation, being either directly or indirectly inter-connected to other elements, has the potential to influence the full range of adoptive inter-relationships.

Adoption is so much more than the static interplay between adoptee, adoptive parent and birth parent. By choosing to utilize the metaphor of the constellation, we are able to see the flow of interactions among all those who are constituent players in the process of adoption. Since all elements in the constellation have "gravitational" pull, it becomes apparent that each has the possibility of shaping the form of the adoption over time. It extends the boundaries of the constellation so that legislators, policy analysts, social theorists and the media become important forces in the shape of the interior of the constellation made up by adoptees, birth and adoptive parents. In short, it opens up possibilities of new ways of thinking about adoption.

CHAPTER 2

THE PRIMAL WOUND AS THEORY

Perhaps no other theoretical perspective has been embraced with as much enthusiasm by the adoption community as has the primal wound theory offered by Nancy Verrier (1993), an adoptive parent. A cursory view of adoption activist web sites and book displays at adoption conferences will indicate that *The Primal Wound* has a place of prominence for those concerned about the effects of adoption on adoptees and their birth parents.

The theory may be outlined as follows: There is an inextricable bond that is formed between child and mother in utero. As a consequence, if the child is separated from the biological mother, the child and the mother will each suffer an irreparable psychic wound. Nothing can repair that wound save for the reformation of the bond between these two beings. Another way of saying this is that adoption is a form of family formation that is doomed to fail. The adoptive family (and especially the adoptive mother) can never take the place of the birth mother in the psychic life of the child. Furthermore, all of the recent initiatives to find better ways of facilitating an adoption and living within an adoptive family will result in failure. They do not address the fundamental, psychological reality of the adoptee, which is that the primary bond between adoptee and birth mother has been broken and that nothing can take the place of this first and foremost attachment relationship. Thus, adoptees and birth mothers are said to be victims of the placement process that has broken asunder the link between them. As such, they are victims of an unnatural and disruptive process that leaves them psychically bleeding. And if there are adoptees and birth mothers who do not fit this profile, they are said to be in denial, having buried these feelings of loss and abandonment and are overcompensating as a means of not facing the pain of this loss of connection.

Many adoptees and birth parents have found this to be a very attractive theory indeed. It captures their strong feelings of loss and rejection. What is more important, the theory provides a strong justification for these feelings. Unlike writings geared for adoptive parents, there are no hearts and flowers. The Primal Wound is for many, the first clear exposé of what it is really like to have been placed for adoption.

While I concur that Verrier's book gives voice to the anguish that many have experienced as adoptees and birth parents, I do take issue with Verrier's **explanation** of this reaction to loss. Validation of a theory requires not only that there be empirical support for its hypotheses but in addition, alternative explanations for the findings, other than those posed by the theory, must be ruled out. I believe that a careful reading of the clinical research literature will lead us to a very different understanding of the pain that Verrier documents so well.

Attachment

The first testing ground for this theory is found in the attachment literature. Primal wound theory predicts that infants, taken from their birth mothers shortly after birth and placed into adoptive families, will be unable to form strong and positive relationships with their adoptive mothers[2]. This failure of secured attachment

---

2 Actually, Verrier (1987) makes a distinction between bonding and attachment. She states, "...almost all adopted children form attachments to their adoptive mothers" (p.83). Note that no definition of this attachment is offered. She then goes on to state, "Bonding, on the other hand, may not be so easily achieved. It implies a profound connection, which is experienced at all levels of human awareness. In the earliest stages of an infant's life, this bond instils the child with a sense of well-being and wholeness necessary to healthy development" (p.83). One is left with the conclusion that Verrier sees attachment and bonding as being at the ends of a dimension of intensity and intimacy. Given

is considered the result of infant conditioning in utero to the bio-rhythms of the birth mother. With separation from her, the child is placed into a bewildering array of sights, smells and sounds that have neither familiarity nor association with safety and security. Hence, the child will show attachment to the adoptive mother that is marked either by insecurity and clinging or distance and un-responsiveness to her parenting attempts. It is further argued that either disorganized or insecure attachment will result in adoptive children developing a future internal working model of relation-ships that will leave them vulnerable to a variety of personal and interpersonal difficulties in later life.

Assessment of the attachment style of infants and their pri-mary care takers provides a good test of the primal wound theory. At this stage of the child's development, this early relationship is unencumbered by the confounding cognitive representations of adoption and attachment that are part of the cultural discourse of adoption. In other words, the infant is predominantly responding to visceral cues that have influence because of their salience in the prenatal period. There is no need to consider what the infant thinks about the replacement caretaker, for the infant is not symbolically coding at this point.

Thus, one would expect when looking at the research evidence that there would be a plethora of data describing the attachment difficulties of young, adopted children. While there is no short-age of articles that theorize such a position, research support for this position is either scant or open to alternative interpretations that account for the findings without having to resort to a Primal Wound explanation.

The first question to be asked is whether there are differential rates of secure versus insecure attachment found in adoptive and non-adoptive families with young infants. In a series of studies

---

that the writings in attachment offer schemas that cover the range of these emotions, her distinction offers little to our understanding of close, early relationships.

carried out in England, Tizard (1977) and Tizard and Hodges, (1978) reported that adopted two year olds were more clingy and displayed more diffuse attachments than did two year olds raised in non adopted homes. Differences continued up to the age of eight when the adopted children were observed to have more social difficulties, were more attention seeking and showed more indiscriminate affection. All of these behaviors are ones that would be expected, based on the Primal Wound Theory. However, before jumping to the conclusion that this represents support for the theory, it should be noted that all of the adopted children in this study were in institutional custodial settings prior to their placement into adopted homes. Thus, we are left with the alternative explanation that their signs of weak attachment are not the result of being placed for adoption but are likely the consequence of their prior placement history in institutions (Verhulst, Althaus, & Versluis-Den Bieman, 1990). Their behavior matches the behavior of children raised in orphanages where diffuse attachment and overt friendliness are adaptive skills that enhance social support and care. What is seen as weakness in an adoptive home is, in reality, a sign of strength and resilience in another setting. The challenge for children initially placed in institutions is to learn that alternative strategies are needed within the adoptive home.

Another study, well cited in the literature, was carried out by Yarrow and Goodwin in 1973. They found that infants, separated from their birth parents after six months of age, displayed signs of maladjustment throughout the following 10 years after placement. Of major concern was their inability to form close social relationships. Again, one is tempted to suggest that this study provides support for Verrier's position. However, good research design demands that the adopted group be compared to a matched group of children who were raised in consanguineous homes. Such a group was not a part of Yarrow and Goodwin's study. Hence, it is unclear whether it is adoption that accounts for these results or other factors such as prenatal history or genetic endowments.

A third study has presented indirect evidence of attachment disorders in adoptees. Grotevant, McRoy and Jenkins (1988) undertook a careful examination of the psychological characteristics of adopted and non-adopted adolescents who were being treated in a psychiatric facility. Grotevant et al reported that 20 percent of the adopted patients were reported to be extraordinarily uncomfortable when held as infants. None of the non-adopted patients were found to display this behavior. Rejection of a comforting parent is thought to be a sign of avoidant attachment. However, before concluding that we have found evidence of attachment disorder in adoptees, it must be stated that this study says very little indeed about the wider population of adoptees who are not being seen for psychiatric treatment. It is also possible that there are significant differences between adoptees in the general population and those who are in need of psychiatric treatment. This comparison unfortunately, was not made. Thus, the Grotevant et al. study fails to shed light on the issue at hand.

In 1985 Singer, Brodzinsky, Steir and Waters compared non-adopted, intra racial adopted infants and interracial adopted infants using the strange situation paradigm to assess the quality of attachment relationships. This is the standard experimental procedure in the study of attachment. The infant first spends time with the parent. The parent then leaves the room and the infant is left alone with a stranger. Most young infants become distressed by this situation. The parent then returns to the room. What the distraught infant does in reaction to the parent's return is used as a measure of attachment relationships. If the infant seeks out the parent and is calmed by contact and then returns to exploring the wider environment, the infant is said to be securely attached. If on the other had, the infant either avoids the parent upon return (avoidant attachment), refuses to leave the parent's side (insecure attachment) or has no seemingly organized response to the parent (diffuse attachment), then the infant is said to show some form of attachment disorder.

The results of the study by Brodzinsky et al are quite clear: There were no differences in the mother-infant attachments for intra racial and non-adopted groups. There were also no differences between the intra racial and the interracial adopted groups. Of further interest was the fact that attachment was unrelated to either age at which the child entered the adoptive home or the number of foster placements prior to entering the adoptive home. These results run contrary to what would have been predicted by the Primal Wound Theory.

Similar findings have been found in a study of children, adopted from Sri Lanka, South Korea and Columbia, and placed into homes in Holland before the age of six months (Juffer & Rosenboom, 1997). Results revealed that 74% of the children were rated as displaying secure attachment at 12 months of age. Neither country of origin nor presence of consanguineous children in the home influenced the findings.

Hence, in the two carefully designed studies of attachment, adopted children show patterns of attachment that do not differ significantly from those displayed by non-adopted children. One might argue, however, that these studies do not tap the subtle nuances of connection between adoptees and their adoptive mothers. To this challenge, I concur that better paradigms to measure attachment are needed. That being said, at least one is on firm ground to argue that there is nothing in the research on infant attachment behavior that would currently support Verrier's position.

An alternative way of looking at early adoptive relationships is to turn them around and ask whether adoptive parents experience more distress and maladjustment during the first year after placement than do biological parents with their infants. After all, since Verrier has stated that all adopted infants will not bond with the adoptive parents, it would be expected that adoptive parents would be troubled by these strained parent-child relationships and their distress might be expected to affect their marital relationship.

The research evidence again proves otherwise. A detailed study by Plomin and DeFries (1985) examined the quality of the home environment and the social-emotional relationships of family members when the children were 12 and 24 months of age. Comparing adoptive and biological families, they found no major statistical differences between the groups. Hoopes (1982) reported that adoptive couples felt that they had less marital conflict and more ease of family relationships during infancy and the preschool years than did non-adoptive couples. By the time the children had reached grade school, there were no reported differences between the family types. Humphrey and Kirkwood, (1982) presented similar data. Adoptive couples, with children from infancy through the early teens, reported more positive marital relationships than did non-adoptive couples. Clearly, these studies are not direct tests of the Primal Wound Theory, but they do provide a challenge to the theory. Given the prediction that infants would struggle with connections with the adoptive mother, one would expect to find that these stresses would influence the adoptive mother's mental health. This, in turn, might negatively affect the marital relationship. If anything, these studies would suggest that the opposite occurred. Placement led to better family relations, a result that is hard to imagine if the family is under duress.

Behavioral and Emotional Difficulties.

Turning to another assumption of the theory, Verrier asserts that the Primal Wound is the underlying cause of behavioral and emotional difficulties that adoptees will experience later in life. In response to the tearing apart of the birth mother and child, the child is left with the challenge of responding to the resulting deep pain of loss. This is said to be played out in several ways including depression, acting out, risk taking, inability to form close relationships, anger, aggression or a suppressing of these emotions and becoming the perfect child who never strays beyond the bounds set by the adoptive parents.

On the surface, the research literature matches the outcome that Verrier predicts. Without question, the evidence details more emotional difficulty for adoptees than for those who have not been adopted. However, things are never as simple as they first seem. It is, therefore, necessary to take a more measured look at these findings.

The first question that must be asked is whether children raised in adopted homes are better adjusted than those who raised in institutional settings and foster homes. In detailed studies by Bohman, (1970), Bohman and Sigvardsson, (1990) and Triseliotis and Hill (1990), the results clearly describe adopted children as faring far better than foster or institutionalized children. This speaks well for adoption, although it must be pointed out that there is a possibility that it was not the setting, per se, that accounted for the superior effect of adoption. The competing hypothesis has yet to be ruled out: that children who were placed for adoption were children who were less at risk prior to the placement than were the children raised in the other protection settings. Nevertheless, it would seem that being adopted has some buffering effect that other placement alternatives do not offer.

Often one hears adult adoptees say that they would have fared better in their family of origin than they did in their adoptive home. This observation is clinically assumed to be a sign of mourning not only for the birth family but also for the loss of a personal sense of self that never was given an opportunity to develop within the context of the birth family. While these sentiments are an expected response to having been raised with non consanguineous kin, they contrast with the finding that children who were raised in adoptive homes displayed much more positive long term adjustment than did those who were raised by biological parents who were either equivocal or hostile to the idea of raising their children (Bohman, 1970).

Thus, so far the picture is one in which placement in an adopted home is better for the child than to be in care or remain in a hostile, consanguineous home. Yet, we must still ask whether the psychological profile of adopted children bares any similarity to that of non-adopted children raised in similar socioeconomic circumstances. To foreshadow the results to follow, adoptive status is, indeed, a marker of being at risk for adjustment difficulties. However, two critical questions must be asked: to what degree is this risk apparent; and is the risk the result of being adopted or reflective of other factors that are not directly related to adoption, per se.

Essentially, there are two kinds of studies that assess the degree of risk that adoptees are at for developing emotional adjustment difficulties. The first set of studies looks at whether adoptees are over represented in mental health settings.

While researchers have expressed concern with the quality of demographic data describing the percentage of adoptees in the population (Bachrach, Adams, Sambrano, & London, 1989; Sobol & Daly, 1994) it is generally agreed that adoptees make up between 2% and 4% of the population. When comparing this figure to the percentage of children in clinical settings, it is clear that adoptees are highly over represented: In special education populations, 6.7% are classified as displaying neurological impairment, 5.4% perceptual challenges and 7.2% emotional difficulty (Brodzinsky & Steiger, 1991); approximately 5% of outpatient attendees are adopted (Mech, 1973); and a range of 10 to 15% of child and adolescent inpatients come from adopted homes (Piersma, 1987).

It is easy, using these figures, to jump to the conclusion that the data are consistent with the expectations of the Primal Wound Theory. However, before doing so, it is necessary to ask whether these findings may be the result of factors other than separation from birth parents. One alternative explanation centers on adoptive parents' sensitivity to their child's deviations from behavioral norms. Warren (1992) found that adoptive parents have a lower threshold when it comes to reacting to their children's behavior. This was the case, even when she controlled for the effects of level of behavioral problems. Thus, adoptive parents are more prone to seek out psychological assistance for their children, regardless of the child's level of emotional distress. They are also more likely to attribute misbehavior to biological, internal factors in the children rather than to their own parenting strategies (Cohen, Coyne & Duvall, 1993). Furthermore, given the over representation of upper middle class adoptive parents (Jeffrey, 1992; Daly & Sobol, 1993), it is not surprising that they turn to other middle class professionals for help when their children are in difficulty. After all, these parents are comfortable interacting with professionals in the community. They also were more willing to have their children treated in settings outside of the family than were non-adoptive parents. Together, these findings suggest that adoptive parents are less willing to confront the possibility that they have contributed to the difficulties that their children are experiencing. Externalizing the cause of the problem onto the child lessens a sense of guilt they might have and makes it easier for them to seek assistance from others. Hence, it is not surprising that more adoptees are brought to mental health and educational settings than would be expected, given their numbers in the population.

Another possibility for explaining these results is that adoptees are at risk, not because of their adoptive parents' beliefs and actions or separation from their birth mother, but because they have been exposed to pre and post natal risks that become manifest later in their development. Bohman, (1970) has reported that women, whose infants were placed for adoption, on average, experience more stress over the course of the pregnancy and more complications during the birthing than did women whose infants were not placed for adoption. Thus, it would be expected that these children were exposed to increased levels of stress-related hormones that could have an adverse effect upon their neurological development.

A further prenatal factor that has been shown to have a major effect upon development is that of excessive fetal exposure to alcohol, the outcome of which is fetal alcohol syndrome (FAS). Finkelstein

(1993) and Stevenson (1994) have noted the increased numbers of infants, whose mothers used drugs and alcohol during pregnancy, that have recently been made available for adoption. Many of these infants, regardless of their adoptive status, will develop behavioral and emotional anomalies of a severe nature. The research and clinical challenge, of course, will be to sort out whether adoption serves to moderate or exacerbate the features of FAS and related syndromes.

There is also evidence that adopted children have birth parents who display higher levels of risk for emotional difficulties that have a genetic component (Cadoret, 1990; Loehlin, Willerman & Horn, 1982). This genetic risk would play itself out as temperamental and emotional challenges for their adopted offspring. One could argue that these genetic dispositions interact with separation from the birth mother, a position that I do not think Verrier would have any difficulty with. However, a more parsimonious explanation would leave the explanation at the genetic level. Clearly, more research is needed.

The next question to ask is whether adoptees, seen in mental health facilities, display a unique pattern of symptomatology that distinguishes them from their peers who have lived in different family constellations. With few exceptions, the research literature documents no differences between adopted and non adopted in-patients for mood disorders (Kotsopoulos, Cote, Joseph, Pentland, Stavrakki, Sheahan, & Oke, 1988; Piersma, 1987; Weiss, 1985), conduct disorders (Piersma, 1987), psychosis (Goldberg & Wolkind, 1992), anxiety (Rogeness, Hoppe, Macedo, Rischer, & Harris, (1988), substance abuse, dependency and personality disorders (Weiss, 1985). Again these results call into question the validity of the Primal Wound theory. One would expect that if all adoptees were traumatized by early separation, then a unique constellation of symptoms would mark them off from others who had not ex-perienced such a trauma. However, the research would not support such a position. When adoptees do display evidence of extreme emotional impairment, they are found all over the psychological map, as is the case for their non-adopted peers.

Haugaard (1998) has offered an important caveat about much of the research on psychopathology in adoptee samples. Rarely when conducting these studies, do researchers take into account such factors as age at placement, age at time of assessment, prenatal and post natal history, sex of child, and kind of adoption (step vs. non step). Hence, while trends would indicate that adoptees do appear at higher rates in mental health settings than do non adoptees, it is still not clear whether these results could be better accounted for by attending to the control variables listed above than the child's adoptive status. Hopefully, future research will shed more light on the effects of these variables.

What of non-clinical populations? Are there higher rates of maladjustment in adoptive than non-adoptive samples? A scan of the literature would leave us with the conclusion, "it depends." For the most part, early development is a time when there is little that differentiates adoptees from their non-adopted cohort (Brodzinsky, 1993). However, throughout the primary school years, when adoptees are beginning to fathom the meaning of adoption and loss, there seems to be increased difficulty in meeting the challenges of school, family and social life (Brodzinsky, Lang & Smith, 1995). For example, Brodzinsky, Radice, Huffman and Merkler (1987) reported that compared to a matched non adopted cohort, adopted boys displayed significantly more uncommunicative behavior (20.0% vs. 4.6%) and hyperactivity (8.2% vs. 0.0%) while adopted girls were given higher ratings for depression (13.9% vs. 3.0%), hyperactivity (13.9% vs. 0.0%) and aggression (10.8% vs. 0.0%).

Before concluding that this represents adjustment difficulties fuelled by separation from birth parents, we must consider the fact that the ratings of the children were made by their adoptive parents. We have already noted that adoptive parents are more prone to see their children's difficulties as dysfunctional than are non-adoptive parents (Warren, 1992). Furthermore, Priel,

Melamed-Hass, Besser and Kantor (2000) found that adoptive parents' ratings of their children's adjustment are partially a function of the parents' degree of self-reflectiveness. This is a characteristic of psychological functioning that emphasizes a parent's ability to differentiate self from others and to be cognizant of the mental state of self and other. Parents with low self-reflectiveness tended to rate their children as having great adjustment difficulties. Thus, it is surprising that so few differences have been found between the adoptees and non-adoptees, given the adoptive parents' proclivity to negatively assess their children. Clearly, before we can draw any strong conclusions about the use of rating scale evaluations of adopted children, we must insure that the raters are blind to the child's family status. The second caution that must be offered is that for the vast majority of adoptive children, the results indicated that they were not displaying significant levels of clinical impairment. The Primal Wound theory would argue that all adopted children suffer from the trauma of separation and loss and hence will display adjustment difficulties. It is hard to reconcile this aspect of the theory with the results found by Brodzinsky et al., (1987).

What of adolescence? Is the alleged storm and stress of this period the setting for adoptee dysfunction? The research literature would suggest otherwise for adolescence is not seen as a period of major turmoil for adoptees (Bohman & Sigvardsson, 1990). Stein & Hoopes, 1985), for example, carefully examined general identity formation of adolescent adoptees and non-adoptees and found no differences in the manner in which the two groups dealt with identity issues. Sobol and Hundleby (1993) analyzed a data set of 1800 teenagers, 56 of whom were adopted (3%), and found that there were no differences between adoptees and those raised in consanguineous homes for sexual behavior, delinquent activity, drug use, school performance or relationships with parents. Interestingly, the group that was at risk for acting out behavior was teens raised in stepparent families.

It would be easy to take these findings and conclude that adoptees have no issues during adolescence. I think this would be erroneous. Adolescence is a time of great challenge for all teens. The fact that adoptees may have an extended agenda for identity formation, however, does not mean that they will not make the adaptive responses needed to determine whom they are, where they have come from and what they wish to become. However, those processes will also require an accommodating home environment and a wider supportive community to recognize the special needs of adoptees, and to assist in the creation of a positive self-narrative.

For now, the findings on adjustment may be summarized as follows. There is evidence that adoptees in middle childhood display some elevation in adjustment difficulties. In infancy, preschool and adolescence, there is little to suggest that as a result of a primal wound, adoptees, as a group, are more at risk than are those raised in consanguineous families. In fact, for a majority of adoptees, regardless of age, there is little evidence to indicate that they are at risk for maladjustment. Nevertheless, this is not to say that adoptees do not feel the pain of loss for birth parents, which might have profound psychological consequences. As Smith and Brodzinsky, (2002) have reported, higher negative affect about birth parent loss was related to higher self reported level of depression and lower self-worth. Being written out of the first chapter of one's life is not a benign event. Clearly, the issue is what one makes of this separation and loss. I will return to this theme in the next chapter.

It is also important to note that other than Smith and Brodzinsky's (2002) study, few researchers have used adoption-specific measures to assess adjustment. Instead, measures of psychopathology or behavioral disturbance, that are not directly reflective of the adoptive experience, are the norm. It is assumed by most researchers that maladjustment of adoptees does not differ from the maladjustment of those who were never adopted. This may account, in part, for the relatively low level of adjustment difficulties reported for adoption. If emotionally sensitive, adoption-specific measures were used that reflected directly the pain of not feeling authentic, loosing birth family and a potential self, and the challenge of living with an incomplete personal narrative, then a different picture of the emotional make-up of adoptees might emerge. Until we see such studies, we should desist from making strong statements about adoptees' adjustment[3].

Another methodological caution comes from Wierzbicki's (1993) meta-analytic review of studies assessing the psychological adjustment of adoptions. Wierzbicki noted that larger differences between adoptee and non-adoptee groups were found in those studies that had small numbers of subjects and used qualitative rather than quantitative measures of assessment. These findings again caution us to be careful when drawing conclusions, as much of our knowledge may be open to sampling and rater bias. Clearly, the jury is still out on this issue.

The Determinacy of the Primal Wound

In spite of the fact that there does not seem to be any strong empirical support for the hypothesized occurrence of a Primal Wound and its effect upon subsequent adjustment, let us assume for the moment that Verrier is correct, and that adoptees do indeed fail to form secure attachments with their adoptive mothers. Why should this be important?

Verrier, following the work of Bowlby (1969, 1973, 1980), suggests that the emotional connection between parent and infant provides a model for the child for all subsequent interpersonal relationships. This working model dictates how close one can fear to tread, how open one can be and what range of emotions can be expressed in the presence of important emotionally-charged

---

3   The same can be said for the research on birthparent long term adaptation to placement of their children. Most studies use conventional measures of psychopathology. However, adoption sensitive measures that tap the full dimension of birthparents' adoptive experiences might yield a contrasting view of placement outcome.

individuals. If the infant does not feel safe with the adoptive mother, rejects her or clings insecurely to her, or worst of all, shows no interest in her, then it is expected that these themes will be played out repeatedly across development with other close individuals. This is a highly determinist aspect of the Primal Wound Theory. One is seen to be a prisoner of the past. Our initial model becomes our lifetime model. We continue to live out our earliest experiences time and time again.

Thus, adoptees and birth mothers are presented by Verrier as victims of a social act that leaves them emotionally bleeding until such time as they are able to reunite and begin to heal this gaping affective wound. Note that the theory does not present modifying statements that recognize that not everyone in adoption will go through a similar process.

What does it mean to be a victim of adoption? Victims are usually thought of as passive and helpless in the face of negative, external forces. Victims are said to be injured or significantly flawed in some fashion by traumatic events that have left them with either physical or psychological scars that frame subsequent experience. Victims also lack a sense of personal agency. Change, relief and healing are not under their personal control and so they must wait for things to happen to them if they are ever to experience a sense of relief from their victim status. The Primal Wound Theory is a psychologically deterministic theory. It posits that adoptees have no choice and their life course is set at that moment after birth when they are physically removed from the birth mother. There is little that can be done to avoid the pain inflicted by the primal wound of separation or the resulting status of victim that shapes their future emotional relationships.

The theory proposes that one's very being is defined exclusively and completely by a specific incident or experience. It follows that one cannot think of oneself in any manner other than in relation to the incident that led to victim status. Furthermore, one cannot have an identity other than that related to being a victim of adoption. No other role or self-identity enters into the picture. One is a victim of adoption and not a child of parents, a teenager with all the accompanying anxiety that this role entails, a young adult choosing a career and a companion for life's journey, a parent and grandparent. One can never just have an identity crisis like other people. One cannot be angry with one's parents or one's children without it being in reaction to the removal of the adoptee from the birth mother. Thus, if one accepts the Primal Wound Theory, one never joins in the community of other people who struggle with life, question their self worth, wonder what their essence might be, argue with parents, search out roots and find a way in life regardless of whether the road is rocky or smooth.

Within other close relationships, modes of interaction are said to be tainted by the fact that adoptee and birth parent are victims. Thus, one is a victim married to a mate, one is a victim who raises a child, and one is a victim who interacts with co-workers. One cannot escape being a victim in relationship with others. One is a helpless individual, devoid of hope, initiative, or joie de vivre across all of life's experiences. To be a victim is to remain in a permanent state of depression and anger.

One of the central premises of the Primal Wound Theory is that *all* adoptees, placed as young infants, are victims. There are no exceptions. If an adoptee does not display the anticipated consequences of this painful separation, either the person is thought to be over compensating for the loss by being exceptionally "normal," or the person is said to be in a state of denial with its own set of constituent, psychological difficulties.

This theory is an example of "continuity" theory (Lewis, 1997). Development is conceptualized as linear. There are clear and direct lines from past to future. Knowing the past comes very close to being able to describe what the future will look like. As a continuity theory, it shares theoretical space with theories such as Piaget's genetic-epistemological theory of cognitive development and Freud's theory of psychosexual development.

Recently, there has been some questioning of the theoretical adequacy of continuity theories. Indices of early experiences and structures are not very robust predictors of future development. For example, knowing the attachment status of a young child does predict future social and emotional relationships, but the question is, to what degree do these measures predict later outcomes. Here we must diverge for a moment to distinguish between statistical significance and proportion of variance accounted for in the relationship. We know that early indices of development are correlated with later indices at around the .40 level. This means that these two variables are systematically related. The relative ranking that one receives on an earlier measure would be somewhat similar to the relative ranking received on a measure taken at a later point in development. Furthermore, this relationship has a low probability of occurring by chance. In other words, they bare some true relationship. This is where most people stop. They are satisfied with knowing that, for example, early attachment is related to later friendship patterns. However, what else do we know from a correlation of .40? Without going into the statistical complexities of the matter, suffice it to say that this correlation accounts for 16% of the variation in the two variables under consideration. What we have not accounted for is the remaining 84% of the variation between them. In other words, one can have a true and reliable relationship, but not be able to explain very much about it. And this is the case with early precursors of future development.

The Primal Wound Theory is based on the premise that by knowing something of the past, the future is accounted for. However, life is never this straight forward. We rarely travel in direct lines from the past to the future. Obstacles and challenges cross our paths. Lewis (1997), in his book, "Altering fate: Why the past does not predict the future," argues persuasively that it is only when the context in which we live our lives remains stable, that early structures remain operative in the future. Yet when the context no longer supports a particular way of being, then the individual is moved into other directions that takes one off the early trajectory of development. Sometimes the context in which one finds oneself pushes the individual toward higher and more adaptive levels of development. At other times, the context turns the person to less adaptive means of coping.

Lewis also argues that one should not think of contextual conditions as mindless forces that shape one's destiny. Instead, he puts forth the notion of personal agency: We are active co-participants in the creation of meaning in our lives. Note that this does not place full responsibility on the shoulders of those in adoption who continue to experience the pain of loss. Lewis is arguing for an explanation that balances the effects of context-as-given with context-as-created by the individual. We are not the prisoners of the past nor are we the creators of the effects of the past alone. Both context and the personal, meaningful, structuring of this context shape the direction of our development. This is an important idea that runs counter to the determinacy of the Primal Wound Theory.

A Narrative Shift

Is there a better way of thinking of oneself than carrying the psychological baggage of victimhood? I believe there is. The challenge is to find a personal narrative that does not have as its central motif the description of oneself as a victim. To accomplish this task, it is not necessary to go very far beyond the limits of the victim narrative. By simply recognizing that one is not a *victim* (as a status) but that one may have been *victimized,* a range of possibilities opens up that does not share psychological space with the victim narrative.

It is important to make a distinction between what it means to be victimized as opposed to being a victim. I use the term "victimized" to describe specific acts that directly attack the individual's sense of well being. Acts of victimization, when committed, fail to respect the integrity of the individual and may result in feelings of belittlement. However, they need not necessarily leave an indelible stain upon the character of the individual. One's character may be altered by acts of victimization but this does not mean that one is necessarily weakened by these experiences.

I will give an example of the difference between victim and victimization by briefly describing a study of women who had been sexually abused as children. Davis (2000) interviewed women who represented different social classes, ethnicities and life experiences. What they all had in common was the experience of having been sexually abused on multiple occasions while they were youngsters. Every one of the women described the events of their youth in painful, emotional terms. All agreed that it had been the worst thing that had ever happened to them. In typical cultural parlance, we would normally refer to these women as victims of sexual abuse. However, many of them stated unequivocally that although the abuse was horrific, they strongly believed that they were different and significantly stronger as a result of having lived through these experiences. Of course, no one ever stated that abuse "builds character." They were simply pointing out that as adults, they had choices to make about how they were to live with their histories. Some could only focus on the pain and loss of innocence. Others created personal narratives with the central motif being that they became stronger as a means of dealing with their painful pasts. Their narratives were marked by resilience and potential. They did not see their lives scripted in only one direction by these early events. They found adaptable self-descriptions, sometimes through therapy, but often through having strong networks of social support.

The AIDS community has also understood this idea of distinguishing between victim and acts of victimization quite well. In the early days of the AIDS epidemic, it was common to refer to people with HIV as "victims of AIDS." Today, there has been a dramatic shift in nomenclature, as this community has recognized that thinking of oneself as a victim does little to further the needs of the community. Now people in these circumstances refer to themselves as "persons living with AIDS."

In the chapters that follow, I will present several examples of acts of victimization in adoption and some of the possible responses to these hurtful experiences.

CHAPTER 3

ADOPTION AND STIGMA

*In response to the question of what it is like to live in the
waters of the deep, the fish replied, "What waters?"*

What is a Family?

What is a family? It seems like such a simple question. In fact,
we rarely ask this question for the answer is so much a part of our
taken-for-granted experience.

In Western culture, family is a concept that is defined as a
collective of individuals who are related by virtue of their shared
genetic material. The more one shares common genetic material,
the closer one is said to be a family relative. Hence, siblings are
closer relatives than are first cousins. Furthermore, family is an
organizing principle for relationships between individuals who
share genetic material. Hence, we say in common parlance, "blood
is thicker than water," that we are closer to family than we are to
individuals who do not share our genetic material. The dictum that
"blood is thicker than water" is seen as a motivating force pushing
us toward caring for our kin before we share our limited resources
with non-kin. It binds parents to children and children to parents,
and ties us to a sense of connection to our genetic ancestors.

This view of family is also conceived of as a natural form. It is
not often considered a social product of a given society but is viewed
as a universal phenomenon. No matter where we go in the world,
we believe we will find groups of people organized into family units
based on shared genetics. After all, if this description of family

relationships, based on genetic connection, is correct, then it could not be otherwise for it is an expression of what it means to be human.

Schneider (1980) also notes that a "relationship that is 'real' or 'true' or 'blood' or 'by birth' can never be severed, whatever its legal position. Legal rights may be lost, but the blood relationship cannot be extinguished. It is **culturally** defined as being an objective fact of nature, of fundamental significance and capable of having profound effects, and its nature cannot be terminated or changed. It follows that it is never possible to have an ex-father or an ex-mother, an ex-sister or an ex-brother, an ex-son or an ex-daughter. An ex-husband or ex-wife is possible, and so is an ex-mother-in-law. But an ex-mother is not . . . " (p.24).

Another aspect of a genetic family relationship is that it serves the purpose of providing an identity. Those who share a genetic endowment claim a common connection that defines who they are as individuals and as relatives. Being of "the same blood," they see in each other commonalities of temperament, appearance, skills, and style. Only genetic relatives are said to share in such an intimate and closely connected fashion. This belief in a genetic, constitutional basis for shared characteristics reinforces a sense of family connectedness, thus supporting the genetic definition of kinship.

Western anthropologists have strengthened the idea of the legitimacy of the genetically connected family by contrasting it with other family forms that they refer to as "fictive" (Schneider, 1980). These are families that put on a face of being a genetically connected family in an attempt to mirror "true" families. Examples of fictive families include step, adoptive, same sex and single parent families. These groupings fall into the fictive category because family is defined by two unrelated individuals coming together to produce offspring who share 50% of their genetic material with each of their progenitors. In single parent, step and same sex families, one of the progenitors is absent either by choice or circumstances. These family forms are thought of as less legitimate than the nuclear genetic family. However, they are considered more legitimate than the adoptive family where no adult in a parenting role shares a genetic connection to the child.

This understanding of what constitutes a family, on the surface seems like it is nothing more than a reflection of nature. After all, the scientific understanding and description of genetic relationships are assumed to be a true mirror of the world as given. Nevertheless, some anthropologists such as Schneider (1980) have recognized that our understanding of what constitutes a family is part of our wider, Western acceptance of the notion that science should serve as a guidepost for social understanding. Thus, if science were to tell us that our genetic description of inherited characteristics was different from what we now believe it to be, then we would more than likely accept whatever new, scientific perspective emerged.

Furthermore, after a careful examination of non-Western family forms, Schneider (1984), in a carefully reasoned analysis, concluded that not every society bases its definition of family on genetic distance between individuals. For some societies, family groups follow other lines that are behaviorally and functionally based (Terrell & Modell, 1994). One becomes a member of a family by acting like a member of the family, regardless of whether the person has a genetic tie to others in the group (Furstenberg, 1995; Lempert, 1999). Since a person had just as much chance of being a close relation by virtue of being an in-law sharing no genetic material, as being a barer of common genetic material, Schneider (1980) concluded that definitions of family are cultural constructs that do not necessarily have to follow genetic lines. In other words, family is whatever we say it is. In the West, family is defined by genetic links or the "blood bond" (Modell, 1994). Hence, in our society, a family is not a "real" or "true" family unless the children share genetic material with the parents.

It is, therefore, not surprising that theoretical concepts such as Verrier's notions of the primal wound and disrupted attachment have received so much currency in discussions of adoption. After all, these perspectives are grounded in wider cultural discourse about what a true family must be. When genetics is thought to define "true" kinship, it is an easy cultural step to describe the parent-child relationship as cemented by a bond of "love and attachment." Adoption, is then deemed to be an institution destined to fail for it represents the removal of the infant from the "real" parents and the placement of the infant with "fictive" kin who are not bound to the child by parental bonds of blood. Of course, all of this is premised on an exclusive acceptance of the genetic definition of kin.

Where does this leave the adoptive family? It depends on whether one is willing to follow Schneider's (1980) lead and accept the position that kinship is a cultural and not a biological artifact. When we do so, there emerges an alternative understanding of the adoptive family. Although not construed as a "real" family in the material and natural sense of being comprised of genetically related kin, the adoptive family does take on legitimacy to the extent that adoptive relatives "have a relationship in the sense of following a pattern of behavior, a code of conduct . . . They are relatives by virtue of their relationship, not their biogenetic attributes" (Schneider, 1980, p.27). That is to say, because the adoptive family enacts functional roles that mirror those found in genetically related families, they will be recognized as having some degree of legitimacy. This, however, raises an interesting paradox. At the same time that the adoptive family strives to appear as a normal family, they fail to recognize and address those unique factors that mark themselves off from consanguineous families. Kirk (1964), many years ago, warned that adoptive families that denied the differences between themselves and consanguineous families would quickly find themselves engaging in dysfunctional patterns of behavior. Examples of positive acknowledgement of difference include a recognition that the adopted child is a member of two families, the birth family and the adoptive family; a nurturing of the skills and aptitudes of the adopted child that may differ from those possessed by the adoptive family; and an acceptance of the adopted child's desire to explore a family history that includes the birth family. Thus, in an effort to be a successfully functioning unit, the adoptive family is caught between not wanting to be labeled as fictive, while at the same time having to address issues that identify them as not being like consanguineous families.

In an attempt to strengthen the legitimacy of the adoption, family law often includes the phrase, " . . . as if born to . . . " in order to make the adoptive parent-child relationship more consistent with prevailing cultural scripts about the factors that define a "real" family. Paradoxically, by including such a phrase to obscure the lack of a genetic connection between parent and child, the non-genetic connection is, in fact, highlighted. Furthermore, this phrase, "as if born to" also writes the child's birth family out of the script and by doing so, again fails to follow Kirk's warning that acknowledgement is better than denial of difference in adoptive families. These however, are not the only challenges to the legitimacy of the adoptive family.

Stigmatization in Adoption
Definition of Stigma.

If the adoptive family is fictive in that it falls outside of the normative view of kinship based on "blood," then adoptive status meets the definition of a stigma, an "attribute that is deeply discrediting" and reduces the bearer "from a whole and usual person to a tainted, discounted one" (Goffman, 1963, p.3). Goffman did not see stigma as lying within an individual or group. Instead, he described the interrelationship between attributes of the targeted person and the stereotype held by the observer. This led Link and Phelan (2001, p.2) to offer a more encompassing definition of stigma:

"...stigma exists when the following interrelated components converge. In the first component, people distinguish and label human differences. In the second, dominant cultural beliefs link labeled persons to undesirable characteristics - to negative stereotypes. In the third, labeled persons are placed in distinct categories so as to accomplish some degree of separation of "us" from "them." In the fourth, labeled persons experience status loss and discrimination that lead to unequal outcomes. Stigmatization is entirely contingent on access to social, economic and political power that allows the identification of differentness, the construction of stereotypes, the separation of labeled persons into distinct categories and the full execution of disapproval, rejection, exclusion and discrimination. Thus, we apply the term stigma when elements of labeling, stereotyping, separation, status loss and discrimination co-occur in a power situation that allows them to unfold."

According to Link and Phelan (2001), there are three levels of stigma-related discrimination. The first level involves direct discrimination. A person holding negative stereotypes about another will use these attitudes and beliefs to form judgments and subsequently to engage in direct forms of overt discrimination toward the other. The second level is that of structural discrimination. In this form of discrimination, no direct, face-to-face action is taken against the stigmatized person or group. However, as a result of the process of stigmatization, social structures, in the form of services, opportunities and social support are less available to the stigmatized person than they are to the non-stigmatized person. The final level of discrimination is that of the social psychological processes operating through the stigmatized one. Here, the stigmatized person internalizes the attitudes, beliefs and stereotypes of the wider community about the stigma. Holding such a world view means that the individual will engage in behaviors that confirm the wider views about self and will display a defensive emotional stance as a means of coping with these negative views. The result is self-defeating affect in the form of depression, anger, passivity and low self-esteem. In other words, the person inadvertently confirms the stigmatizing by others.

The sections that follow will provide a description and elaboration of how this model of stigmatization maps onto the process of adoption.

Distinguishing and Labeling Differences in Adoption.

When we think about differences between individuals and groups, it becomes obvious that some characteristics matter socially more than others. As noted above, being a normative, non-fictive family member does not require that one be a good parent or child, that one share specific physical characteristics or that one have the same skills and aptitudes. All that is required is that the person be related "by blood" to other family members. We simply assume that this is the way things are, that this is a natural imperative. Since we rarely question our definitional positions, we are easily led to engage in simplifying the categorizing of people into real and fictive kin. There are few shades of grey in this process. A person either is or is not a legitimate family member.

One of the consequences of this act of simplification is that there is little recognition of the heterogeneity within categories. This allows writers such as Verrier (1989) to talk of *all* adoptees and their birth mothers as suffering a primal wound of separation. If they were to express little sense of loss for the relationship of origin, they are said to be in state of denial. In other words, once placed within the category of adoptee or birth mother, there is little room for variation in explanation. One model is said to fit all.

This act of simplification is most apparent when we come to examine research in adoption. It is the rare study, indeed, that controls for placement history when examining the effects of adoption for adoptees. Children are brought to placement along many different pathways. Some are infants. Others range up into their early teens. Pre and postnatal histories may challenge the possibility of smooth development. Some children have been physically or sexually abused. Others have had a safe and secure early beginning. Today, most children are coming to adoption following a history of foster and institutional care. Daly and Sobol (1993) reported that more children from overseas were being adopted than were domestic infants. Clearly, we cannot lump all adoptees into one category.

Birth parents also do not make up a homogeneous group. Some mothers are barely into their teens when their children are placed for adoption. Others are much older. Birth parents come from all social strata of society, although there is a preponderance of lower socioeconomic participants. Some birth parents had a choice in whether their children were to be placed. Others had no choice as their children were under the protection of the state. In some adoptions, birth parents are given opportunities to be an active participant in the placement of the child. In other adoptions, they are no more than the progenitor of the child. Again, there is little commonality in the life histories and placement activities of these parents.

This heterogeneity is no different for adoptive parents. While most are married, middle class, Caucasian and have had some higher education (Sobol & Daly, 1993), this description definitely does not fit all adoptive parents. Furthermore, while most approach adoption as childless couples, some who adopt have birth children as well. It is also clear that adoptive parents are motivated by a myriad of factors to adopt. Thus, the characteristics of this group, like the others, do not allow for easy simplifications.

However, in spite of the heterogeneity of these three groups, when defining kinship, all differences are cast aside. Kin are blood-defined and hence, adoptees and adoptive parents are engaged in a fictive relationship. At the same time, we say adoptees and their birth kin are "real" family. In this scheme of things, there is no room for recognizing the possibility that kinship is more than genetic relationship. As one writer described it, "familial relationships are nourished and sustained by the accumulation of thousands of daily acts of support and care" (Washington, 1991, p.38). Such a view does not negate a genetic view of kin but it does open up the possibility that one can be a parent and not necessarily be of the same blood as the child.

Over the past decade or so, there has been a steady shift in the definition of kinship within the adoption community. While previously, in defensive rejection of the wider cultural definition of kin as genetically defined, adoptive parents and professionals stressed behavioral role enactment as the defining characteristic of parenthood. Since birth parents were taken out of the picture, having been legally and socially rejected from partaking in the ongoing life of the adoptive family, they were excluded from publically claiming parental status. However, with growing acceptance of openness in placement and beyond, we see a shift in the definition of parenthood. At least within the adoption community there is some movement toward defining parenthood as both genetically and behaviorally driven. It is not a matter of saying that one parent is real and the other is fictive. They are both real. They are different by virtue of the degree of involvement and salience that each has in the life of the adoptee at any given time. Extending the definition of parenthood does not necessarily have to diminish the position of either parent. What is clear, though, is that movement in the definition of kin within the adoption constellation is not matched by a similar consideration of kin within the wider society.

Human Differences and Negative Attributes.

The next step in the process of stigmatization is the joining of statements of difference to negative or undesirable attributes. That is, once a person or group has been labeled as different from the norm, they are then seen to possess a wider set of negative characteristics pertaining to the difference label. This is commonly referred to as a stereotype.

The normative standard for pregnant women is that they will keep their offspring and raise them. By definition, birth mothers are seen to be outside of the bounds of this definition of parent in that they do not have legal entitlement to raise their children. Whether loss of parental rights was voluntary or coerced is almost irrelevant. It is the fact that they are not engaged in the behavioral role enactment of parenting that marks them as different. And how does this play out as a stereotype? Birth mothers are typically seen as "fallen women"[4] (Shalev, 1989). This seems to apply regardless of what the circumstances were that led to the pregnancy in the first place. The male's contribution to the pregnancy is rarely, if ever, recognized. It does not seem to matter whether she became pregnant as a result of rape, abuse or inadequate contraception. All that matters is that she became pregnant, gave birth and did not raise her child. Since parents are normatively defined as the genetic progenitors of their children, the non fulfillment of the active parenting role is enough to say that birth mothers have broken natural law and it is this that marks them in the eyes of society as immoral (Miall, 1996).

Finally, in an era in which moral and mental health are rarely seen as synonymous, there is some shift away from the concept of the "fallen woman" toward the perception of the mentally ill person who lacks the insight, emotional fortitude and courage to parent the child. Hence, "choosing to give up the child" is then characterized as evidence of mental disturbance.

Adoptees are also stereotyped. To be the offspring of an immoral parent is to be considered morally tainted oneself. We are not that far away from the commonly held societal view that adoptees were the "devil's spawn." Also, the perception that adoptees have been "given away" implies that there was something about them that made them objectionable enough not to be kept by their birth parents. This stereotype is held in the face of the fact that few children were ever simply "given away." For most, the life circumstances and lack of social support offered to the birth mother accounted for the eventual placement of the child (Sobol & Daly, 1992). It was nothing about the child per se, yet the stereotype of tainted goods persists. This is played out most forcefully when we recognize the widely held belief that most adoptees are maladjusted individuals.

---

4   This phrase and others to follow have been placed in quotations to indicate that the words represent typical, societal discourse about adoption. The meaning of the phrase, however, does not always reflect the lived experience of the parties to an adoption.

Unfortunately, this attitude has been encouraged by some members of the adoption activist community who, when encountering emotional difficulties of adoptees, posit a reason for disparaging the institution of adoption. Of course, as has already been noted, the evidence for adoptee maladjustment is far less wide spread than is usually portrayed. When pre and postnatal factors unrelated to adoption and familial conditions are factored out, the degree of emotional adjustment is radically reduced, and yet the stereotype persists.

Secrecy about origins of the adoptee also contributes to the stereotyping of adoptees. After all, if there were nothing bad to hide, why would records or conversations about origins be closed? Lack of access to information about one's genetic heritage raises questions about the possibility that the child's origins began within the context of rape, abuse, drugs or mental illness. The assumption is that if the child's origins reflected strength and integrity then one's beginnings would be celebrated and not hidden.

The adopting couple is also not free from stigma. In our society, being childless is thought of as a selfish act. When couples do not have children, they are first seen as narcissistically focused on their own needs and uninterested or incapable of responding to the needs of future offspring. However, with time, it is often suspected that childlessness is not an option of choice, and that for the couple (or more likely the woman) is thought to be infertile. In the first case, these couples are seen as turning their backs on what is perceived to be the natural role of fertile couples. In the second, they are viewed as biologically deficient, as not having children puts their fertility challenges on display for all to see (Kessierer & Bryant, 1996). What is apparent in both scenarios is that they, personally, are stigmatized by their childlessness.

Couples who wish to parent a child will go to great lengths before turning to adoption. Almost universally, their first choice is to have their own genetic offspring (Daly, 1988). Following a period of attempting to conceive without the assistance of external intervention, many couples seek medical help. Again, their goal is to produce a consanguineous child. In the past, this sent a very clear message: adoption was second best (Miall, 1996). One would never choose such an option if conception was a possibility. Or, at the very least, one would not wish to adopt before giving birth to one's own genetically related child.

Today, the situation stigmatizes adoption even further. Before choosing adoption, childless couples have more options to consider besides in vitro fertilization (where egg and sperm are united externally and the resulting gamete is then implanted into the woman). Choices abound including donor insemination, egg donation and even the possibility of gamete adoption (where neither member of the couple is genetically related to the gamete). And the choices go on. Surrogate women are being used to carry gametes to term for childless couples where the gamete may or may not be partially or fully related to the couple. In some cases, the surrogate contributes not only a womb but also an egg. In other cases, she just rents her womb for the period of gestation. None of these options is an easy choice. Each is fraught with ethical, medical and financial challenges, but they are indicative of how far couples will go before turning to adoption as a means of forming a family. The resulting message is clear. Adoption is not a preferred choice. It is definitely not the first choice. In fact, it is often the last choice. Being the least favored option for a majority of childless couples is hardly a ringing endorsement of this form of family formation. By their actions, no matter what their intentions, those who take the long route to adoption contribute to its stigmatization.

And physicians are not off the hook, for they too contribute to the disparagement of adoption. Rarely does one find educational and informational material in the offices of fertility specialists that presents adoption as a possible choice for infertile couples. Highlighting the importance of genetic connection, they indirectly contribute to the understanding of adoption as a deficient option (Lebner, 2000). If the question of best interests arises, it is usually asked in reference to the needs of infertile couples. What one rarely hears are concerns voiced about the best interests of the resulting offspring. Furthermore, family practitioners and obstetricians who facilitate adoptions have done so in a closed manner that offers little opportunity to include the birth family in their family and adoption narratives (Daly & Sobol, 1993). Clearly, the medical profession has offered little to enhance the reputation of adoption.

Us and Them.

The next step in the process of stigmatization is the use of social labels to differentiate "us" from "them." Labeled groups are seen to possess negative characteristics. Those who assign these labels believe they, themselves, do not possess similar attributes. As a result, the out-group comes to be perceived as a different type than are the labelers. In the extreme case, those labeled become one-dimensional in that they are seen to be no more than the label itself.

We have three examples of this in adoption: One is not a person whose child has been placed for adoption but is a birth parent; a person who has been adopted is an adoptee; and those persons who adopt are adoptive parents. In each case, much of one's identity is linguistically bound up in the role one is assigned in the adoption drama. While this might be appropriate to the extent that it describes a set of experiences common to the role, it also is limiting. People are more than a circumscribed set of role expectations. They go through life doing many things that have nothing to do with their role assignment in adoption. However, once one is seen to be what the label represents, it is hard to be anything else. An example will make this clear. Recently, the adult child of an important government official in Canada was arrested on a serious criminal charge. In the subsequent news stories, he was referred to as the "adopted son of . . . " even though his adoptive status had absolutely nothing to do with the charge at hand. Clearly this reflects society's stigmatization of those who fulfill roles within adoption. Once labeled, the tag becomes a difficult moniker to shed.

This differentiation of "us" and "them" is also played out when different groups compete for a particular role assignment. In adoption, birth parent and adoptive parent compete for who will be considered the "real" parent. This competition not only takes place at a micro level within a given family but also becomes part of the wider, macro-level labeling of parents. Because stigma results in an "us and them" mentality, there is little room for the consideration of the possibility that both those who gave birth to children and those who have adopted them are the "real" parents. Granted, what that reality might mean depends on the lived experiences of the players. Nevertheless, there is no reason that the two groups must necessarily compete for the role of parent. Sharing the role of "real" parent would require that we think differently on both the interpersonal and the societal level about the definition of parent. Accepting the proposition that kinship is a socially constructed concept, amenable to dialogue and debate, would do much to facilitate the opening of this process.

Status Loss and Discrimination

Link and Phelan (2001) reason that " . . . when people are labeled, set apart, and linked to undesirable characteristics, a rationale is constructed for devaluing, rejecting and excluding them (p.4)." In adoption, these acts of discrimination toward members of the inner orbit of the constellation appear in several forms. They are found in the legislation that manages the definition of family and legitimizes adoption as a legal entity. They are also elaborated in the policies and procedures that serve to implement the intent of the law. These put flesh and bone on the legislation and in many ways are far more effective in managing adoption-related behavior than the more abstract tenets of adoption law per se.

One cannot think of discrimination without considering the unequal distribution of power between those who control aspects of adoption and those whose lives are shaped by the display of this power. It is next to impossible to engage in acts of discrimination without access to power which insures that one can affect an outcome. The powerless are simply not in a position to discriminate against others. They may hold disparaging views. They may act in a hostile fashion toward those whom they believe have wronged them. However, without access to those resources which shape the lives of others, those who are powerless will be unable to actively discriminate.

Finally, it is important to note that discrimination as a process of devaluing, rejecting and excluding is, in fact, a set of discrete acts of victimizing others, of attempting to make them helpless and of placing them under the control of the powerful. Whether by choice or by circumstance, when one is a part of a system of family formation that runs so contrary to the prevailing genetically-based definition of kinship, acts of victimization are likely to occur. Unfortunately, one does not have to look far for examples of such structural discrimination[5].

Whose best interests?

If a child is placed for adoption in circumstances where more consideration is given to the needs of others than to the needs of the birth mother[6] and her child, then a double act of victimization has occurred. The typical birth mother, whose child is not in protective care prior to the placement, is less than 20 years of age, single and poor (Daly & Sobol, 1994). She rarely finds herself

---

5   Link and Phelan (2001) point out two other kinds of discrimination that are experienced by those who have been stigmatized. The first is direct discrimination in which the labeller personally discriminates against the person being labelled. The second form of discrimination is self discrimination whereby the person labelled internalizes the stigma and responds to self as a damaged identity. These will be considered within the adoption context in the following chapter.

6   I have chosen to refer to birth mothers and not birth parent for the simple reason that so few birth fathers seem to participate in the decisions around placement. This may be due to their voluntary withdrawal from the process, their lack or knowledge that they have fathered a child or the fact that facilitators and birth mothers have actively excluded them.

in circumstances where she can easily access the resources necessary to raise a child. Few birth mothers have had experience dealing from a position of equal power with those who wish to place her infant. Not all jurisdictions require by law that the birth mother receive unbiased counseling where alternatives other than placement are considered. It is the rare circumstance where the person offering the counseling to the birth mother is not also the individual offering counseling to the adopting parents. Surely, there is a conflict of interest here. Isolated and vulnerable, some birth mothers may find themselves being forced into making decisions not of their choosing. As a society, we have a responsibility to ensure that decisions around placement are neither coerced nor based upon a consideration of limited alternatives. Placement must not be in the service of meeting the needs of adopting couples wanting to parent a child. One can have compassion for those who have fertility challenges but their needs cannot supersede the needs of the infant and the birth mother.

Finally, a word about the infant: We must look to England to find the case in which the child has an independent counselor whose responsibility it is to insure that the child's best interests are reflected in the decisions around the placement. This person must undertake this role in a manner that places distance between the child's and other individuals' vested interests.

In summary, poorly implemented placements are at risk of exploiting the vulnerability and powerlessness of birth parent and infant. When we carry out such placements, we have committed acts of victimization that limit the best interests of mother and child.

Marketing of Adoptable Children.

It has been estimated that there are approximately a quarter of a million children who are legally eligible for adoption in North America. In the not so distant past, most of these children would not have been considered good candidates for adoption as they possess attributes that were said to make them "hard-to-place": They are older; are part of a sibling group; they may have been exposed to drugs and alcohol during gestation; they may display attention deficit hyperactivity disorder; they may have been physically, sexually or emotionally abused; and they may show aspects of physical, cognitive or emotional impairment. However, two recent factors have led to these children now being viewed as adoptable.

The first factor is the dramatic drop in the number of healthy, Caucasian infants who are being brought forward for adoption. In many parts of Western Europe and North American, infant adoption has either virtually disappeared or has become a small proportion of total adoption placements (Sobol & Daly, 1992). Several hypotheses have been offered for why fewer infants are available for adoption but the argument most in vogue is that the ease of obtaining an abortion is responsible for this drop in number. However, a careful analysis of the demographic data would suggest otherwise (Sobol & Daly, 1992). Today, there are fewer infants available for adoption because more young, single women who find themselves pregnant are choosing to raise their children. Increased social support for this option in the form of daycare, educational opportunities and financial assistance has played some part in the decision not to place. Also, unmarried, single parenthood is simply no longer judged to be inappropriate by a majority of today's society. Hence, within the cohort of young, unmarried women under the age of 24 years, there has been a steady drop in both the rates of adoption and abortion and a matched increase in the number of this cohort who are raising their children (Sobol & Daly, 1994). At the same time, couples who have put off childbearing soon discover that fertility rates go down with age. For many, their plans to have progeny are confounded by the biological reality of a fertility clock that has run its course. Thus, with a growing number of adults seeking to adopt, there is clearly social pressure to make more children available for adoption from other sources. Some have sought out children from overseas but others have looked to the domestic scene. This economic metaphor of supply and demand may not be a comfortable one for many within the constellation.

However, it remains a fact that market forces of greater demand and lesser supply have resulted in the bringing forward of a new group of children for adoption: older children with challenging developmental trajectories.

The second reason we are seeing a shift in the definition of those who are considered to be eligible for adoption is that there has been a dramatic change in North American political-economic culture over the past two decades. Conservative governments have become the norm. Their ascendency has been accompanied by a dramatic cut in the financial support for human services. Strategies have been put in place that have shifted responsibility for services from governmental to personal auspices. One of the casualties of this trend has been a major scaling back of support for protective services for children. Governments are no longer willing to provide the necessary infrastructure to support and preserve families in difficulty. When children from these families are taken into care, again there is little motivation to provide expensive, long-term foster or institutional care. And what is the solution that is offered? It is to move these children off the roster of government-financed support services. In the province of Ontario, for example, legislation has been passed limiting the length of time that children may remain in foster care. Since they are legally severed from their families, the only solution at the end of the fostering period is to place them in adoptive homes. This relieves the state of a major financial burden. They no longer need to pay for the upkeep of these children, beyond the subsidies given to adoptive parents to meet the child's special needs. These subsidies rarely approach the sums set aside to pay for foster care and related child oriented services.[7]

---

7   The disparity between support for adoptive and foster families in terms of subsidies is grounded in the prevailing cultural narrative around family. Foster families are not considered real families. They are agents of the state who stand "in locus parentis" on behalf of the state. They do not have financial responsibility for the child by virtue of the fact that they are not the "real" parents of the child. The state assumes this role.

Of course, told from the governmental perspective, a much higher principle than cost saving is said to motivate their actions. The argument is made that these children deserve permanent, loving homes. Foster care is seen as an impermanent solution that is only slightly better than institutional care but far less appropriate than adoption. Thus, governments say that they are only trying to do what is best for the child. Interestingly, this push to move special needs children into adoptive homes comes at the same time that governments are attempting to make major reductions in their budgets. Coincidence? Perhaps.

Since the early 1980's, we have seen a steady increase in the number of special needs adoptions. In fact, by the beginning of the 1990's, they outnumbered infant placements in Canada by two to one (Daly & Sobol, 1993). Nevertheless, this has not significantly affected the total number of children who remain wards of the state. It has always been the belief of those responsible for the placement of these children that the low rate of placements relative to the number of children in care is the result of a failure to get prospective adopters to consider special needs children. In an attempt to find more adoptive homes for these children, governments and agencies have turned first to newspaper advertising of children and recently, to the use of the internet as a medium for informing the public of the availability for adoption of children with special needs[8]. Children's pictures, developmental history,

---

In the case of adoptive families, the state considered the adopted children to be as if born to the adoptive parents. Hence, financial responsibilities for meeting the child's special needs should be primarily born by the adoptive parents. Note, the paradox. In societal terms, the adoptive parents are considered to be fictive kin. However, when it comes to who shall assume financially responsibility for the children, adoptive parents are considered by the government to be real kin.

8   In some parts of the United States, things have gone even further. Adoptable children are placed on public display at fashion shows and picnics where potential adopters have an opportunity to observe and consider several children over a brief period of time. Many of the children have made repeat appearances at these events without being "chosen." One can only imagine the humiliation and

as well as health and psychological status, are typically part of the display. Potential adopters are encouraged to contact the advertising agent to inquire about their suitability to adopt a child that they are interested in. Major adoptive parent associations such as the North American Council on Adoptable Children and the Adoption Council of Canada have been most supportive of this initiative. They argue that these children need adoptive homes and that it is only a lack of awareness of their availability that stops potential adopters from initiating a placement by making themselves known to placement facilitators.

If this is an allegedly successful strategy for placing adoptees with special needs[9], then why has this issue generated so much opposition from adoptee, birth parent, child advocacy and privacy groups? Is this just one more example of adult adoptees and birth parents having unresolved "emotional baggage" from their own placement history? While many do have strong feelings about the circumstances that led to their personal introduction to adoption, to attribute their opposition to advertising as a sign of emotional disturbance, is to focus off the issue of whether advertising serves the best interests of children with special needs. It also hinders a consideration of other factors that might account for the difficulty in placing these children.

The primary argument that critics of photo listing offer is that it diminishes the integrity of children by treating them as commodities, displayed in the public marketplace, with the expectation of their eventual distribution amongst potential adopters. When a child is put on display, there is rarely any means used to restrict

---

disappoint they must go through, all in the service of finding them permanent homes. Nevertheless, the justification that is offered for this practice is that it serves the best interests of the child.

9   As of the time of the writing of this book, there have been no studies that have carefully and systematically demonstrated that advertising has led to higher placement rates than would occur without wide spread public display of eligible children.

who can gain access to the web site. In a few cases, those wishing to view pictures and receive information about the child's developmental history and current status are first required to register with the listing agency. They are then granted access to the site. However, no site in Canada actively evaluates the intent or background of those wishing to view the children. It is just as easy for pedophiles or classmates to view the contents of these sites as it is for legitimate potential adopters. With such few and loose restrictions, the child's personal and developmental history, psychological and medical status and their picture are there for all to see. More personal material is put on the web than would be found on eBay.

What of consent? Do children have the legal right to decide whether to have their picture, and the fact that they are no longer a legal member of their birth family placed into the public domain? The legal definition of consent requires that the individual be competent to understand the implications of what it would mean to offer consent. How many children whose consent is sought understand that putting their file on the web is not just about finding them an adoptive home? It means that their classmates will gain easy access to personal and private information about them. It means that those who would use the information for illegal and immoral practices will not be denied access to the site. Are young children told that the stigma of public display will stay with them many years after a placement?

It is not surprising that a major source of criticism has come from adult adoptees, many of whom, when they were young, had their pictures and personal stories placed in newspaper advertisements designed to solicit the interest of potential adopters. They know first hand what it means to receive such public exposure. Yet, the rationale provided is always the same: "Yes, but photo listing will attract more people to consider adopting children who otherwise would languish in the foster care system." This response is supported by research indicating that children fare better in adoptive than foster care homes (Triseliotis & Hill, 1990). Therefore, this would be a strong response but only if it could be documented that children with special needs are not being placed because there is a dearth of potential applicants available to adopt them.

This is where the photo listing advocates' argument breaks down. There is simply no documented evidence that these children remain in foster care because there are no suitable and available adoptive homes for them to go to. Agencies have long lists of applicants for adoption. In Canada, on average, it takes seven years to adopt a child from a public or governmental administered facility (Daly & Sobol, 1993). It is almost impossible today to go to a gathering of those seeking to adopt and not hear the following story: "The agency was approached; we expressed our interest in adopting an older child; we filled out some forms; we went to an orientation meeting with others who were also interested in adopting a child with special needs; we never heard from the agency again." Unfortunately, agencies have focused far too long on the placement of healthy infants. This would have been appropriate thirty years ago when the demographics of adoption still tilted toward a large cohort of infants in need of placement. However, today, the majority of children available for adoption have special needs and yet, public agencies have failed to shift their priorities to meet this changing demographic trend. Few systems have been developed to expedite the matching of children's needs and applicants' characteristics and skills. Why are there neither province-wide nor national strategies in place to find these children appropriate homes? Adoption may be a state/provincially-mandated responsibility but placing these children should be a national priority. Furthermore, the past two decades have seen major cutbacks in the financial support for children's services. Our legislators do not want children with special needs to remain the responsibility of the state, yet they are unwilling to adequately fund long term support after these children are adopted. Clearly, politicians have to be called to account. If they wish to transfer responsibility for children with special needs from the public to the private domain of adoptive families, then they must develop and maintain the infrastructure for support services.

The National Adoption Study (Daly & Sobol, 1993) documented some agencies that considered it their mission to place children with special needs into adoptive homes. Staff was well trained in facilitating such adoptions. They were not part of generic protection services but individuals who specialized in this type of adoption. No child was considered unadoptable. Follow-up programs, subsidies and respite care were put into place to assist adoptive parents in caring for their children. Agencies from adjacent jurisdictions met regularly for training and exchange of lists of potential adopters. And perhaps of most importance from the standpoint of placement, applicants were not left dangling, waiting for a response from the agency. Follow-up of applicants was an integral part of the mission of the agencies' adoption program.

Thus, considering the potential harm of photo listing and the clear need to change organizational culture around the placement of children with special needs, it is time to take a step away from the technology of the web. It may be trendy to have a web site and be able to expose these children widely to all and sundry. However, it will have little positive effect until such time as placement of children with special needs is taken seriously at the agency and inter-agency level. Only then will we see these children move away from the impermanence of foster care.

If you are still not convinced of the inappropriateness of photo listing, try thinking about the following possibility[10]. Since adoptive parent organizations are at the forefront of advocating for photo listing, let us just shift the content of the web. Put pictures of those who wish to adopt on the site. However, since we are interested in their best interests, there is no need to seek their consent to do so. Include personal information about fertility status, family composition, financial and health status, personal interests and

10 This idea was suggested to me by Cecelia Reekie, former co-president of the Forget Me Not Society of British Columbia.

attributes. Do not forget to mention that they are "attractive" or "fun loving." Also include a video clip of the applicants splashing away in a pool or being interviewed about their favorite television show. Of course, there will be no restrictions on who can visit this web site or view its contents. Along with their neighbors, friends, family and the general public, we will ask children, who are in foster care, to visit the site. If by chance they see applicants whom they are interested in, they can inform their social worker who will then begin an assessment as to whether those who have been chosen would make good adoptive parents.

Such a reversing of roles would surely gain few adherents. However, it does illustrate what a violation of the person, photo listing can be. If we want to see children with special needs in adoptive homes, let us insure that there are effective systems in place to do so. We do not need more exposure on the web. What we do need are professional practices that do not create a bottle-neck at the agency front door, blocking the appropriate matching of adoptees and adopters.

Relinquishment as a Victimizing Act of Discrimination

One of the most powerful acts of victimization is to label the severing of ties between birth mother and child as "relinquish-ment." Yes, the act of placement does begin the process of breaking the legal connection between mother and child. Adoption does mean, amongst other things, the transfer of parental rights. Many jurisdictions refer to the adopted child "as if born to the adoptive parents." But relinquishment is used in a much wider sense than the breaking of legal ties and responsibilities. We ask birth moth-ers to "get on with their lives, and to get over it." We demand of them that they relinquish all ties to the child, emotional, cogni-tive and social. Interestingly, in my journeys through the adoption community, I rarely hear birth parents and adoptees use the term relinquishment. It is only in groups of adoptive parents that the term comes up with any frequency. Could it be that this reflects their hope that indeed, birth mothers have broken their connection to the child and that the adoptive family need never fear her reappearance in the future?

There is another variation on this theme. In the past, one almost never heard from birth parents and adoptees who did not buy into the cultural discourse on benign adoption. Their public voices were silent. This led advocates of the status quo to use this silence as evidence that, indeed, birth parents not only relinquished legal rights but that they also relinquished their psychological ties to the child. However, in the past decade, new voices have been heard. Groups like Bastard Nation in the USA and The Canadian Council of Natural Mothers have spoken out forcefully about the harm that adoption, as currently practiced, has done to many. And what has been the reaction to this message? Birth parent and adoptee activists are labeled as " carrying emotional baggage" or "having issues." Protest is seen as a marker of psychopathology. After all, the argument goes, true relinquishers do not have issues. Their child was "as if never born to them." This disparaging of dissenting voices is another example of an act of victimization. It is an attempt to negate the lived experience of others who do not fit into the prevailing model of adoption. It does not respect alternative views. It belittles the source of these views and of most importance, it leaves those who take a contrary position feeling angry and frustrated that their voices are either silenced or echoed back to them as pathology. Caught in a no-win situation where either one remains silent or is disparaged for speaking out, is it any wonder that some birth parents and adult adoptees feel a profound sense of helplessness? To say that this sense is only the result of early separation of parent and child is to let others off the hook for their acts of discrimination.

Entitlement to an Accurate History.

At the bedrock of adoption practice, we find attempts to establish the adoptive family as a legitimate concept that is figuratively, if not literally, tied together by a sense of blood. If this were not the case, then we would need to ask why the notion of the adoptive child "as if born to the adoptive parents" has been written into adoption law. To strengthen the myth of consanguinity, original birth records are sealed and a substitute document is made available which names the adoptive parents as the biological parents of the child. While there is no restriction to access to this nonveridical document, in most jurisdictions, access to the original birth registration is either denied to adult adoptees or is allowed only if the birth parent has not placed an information veto on the record. The case often presented for granting such a veto is either that the birth parent had been promised confidentiality as a condition of agreeing to placement, or that identifying knowledge of the birth parents would jeopardize their social standing within their circle of family and friends.

It has not been that long since the act of bringing a child into the world as a single mother was marked by shame and social disapproval. The child was referred to as a bastard and the word "illegitimate" appeared on the birth registration. Young women were sent off to maternity homes that provided a shelter from the censoring eyes of society. Following the birth of the infant, mother and child were quickly separated and the infant was bundled off to the waiting arms of expectant adoptive parents. Birth mothers signed documents severing all legal ties to the child. Counseling, if it was offered, stressed the need for the birth mother to get past the pain of placement, and to make a new life for herself as if the birth and subsequent adoption had never occurred. It was time to wipe the slate clean and to begin afresh.

Seen in this light, closed records would seem to make sense in that they were said to serve the emotional and social needs of birth parents. Or did they? It all depends on whether the history of placement just described, in fact, represented the experiences of those women whose children were placed for adoption.

If one follows the plain meaning of the language of placement, it would seem that all placements were voluntary and birth mothers were fully and accurately informed. We often hear expressions of this sentiment such as "she placed her child for adoption." On the surface, the straightforward meaning of this phrase is that the birth mother took an active role in the placement of her child. She was the agent of transfer, and as such she must have been acting in a volitional and unforced manner. That may have been the case for some. However, for other birth mothers, nothing could have been farther from the truth. It is hard to imagine an active and voluntary placement if the mother either was under the influence of pain medication immediately following the birth or experiencing the flood of post natal hormones that alter mood and impair judgment. Even if the birth mother's cognitive processes were not hindered by drugs or hormones, events following a birth are rarely a time when one is able to make rational decisions. It is a time of heightened emotion and one that is not easily amenable to life-course decisions. Is it, therefore, any wonder that birth mothers often report that they cannot remember ever signing release documents severing their legal connection to their children?

Some birth mothers allowed the placement to proceed, not because they had been promised lifelong anonymity but because they were assured that they would be able to find their children when the infant became a legal adult. Given the state of the law banning easy access to identifying information, this is hardly evidence of informed consent.

And were birth mothers aware of options other than placement? There is no documented evidence that once the wheels were put in motion, any option other than placement was ever pursued with equal vigor by those helping to facilitate the adoption. This is not surprising. The birth mother was viewed as immoral as evidenced by the fact that she found herself in the circumstance of giving birth to a child outside of marriage. In this narrative, the events that led to the pregnancy were considered irrelevant. Rape, incest, and failed birth control were equivalent factors. The only important issue was that she had committed the sin of being pregnant outside of the normative cultural script for birthing. For this, she would have to pay the social price: lost parental rights and the blocking of legal access to identifying information.

However, sealed records were put into place, not just to punish the birth mother, and at the same time, to protect her from a soiled identity. They were also used to meet the needs of adoptive parents.

Again, we must begin with a consideration of our cultural understanding of family. Clearly, adoptive families are at a disadvantage. They are publically recognized as not fitting the prevailing definition of family consisting of a heterosexual couple with consanguineous offspring. A cynic would say, though, that they serve an important function in society for they provide a setting to care for children who have been legally severed from their families of birth. The reasons for the severance are of little importance. These children either are in transition or have already become wards of the state and, as such, are seen to take up valuable communal resources. By encouraging adoption, it is assumed that everyone wins. The state frees itself of the responsibilities for the child. The birth family is divested of any obligations to the child for they have legally relinquished their kin. And most importantly for adoptive applicants, welcoming the child into their home allows them to gain some societal legitimacy for becoming a complete family in the sense that there are now parents and children under the same roof. However, as this is still seen to be a fictive family, without the usual supports of a "legitimate" family, it has been deemed necessary by legislators to find a way to lessen perceived threats to the adoptive family. And what is the primary threat to this family presumed to be? It is the possibility that the birth family will encroach on the life of the adoptive family through reconnection with the adopted child. Since it does not matter whether adoptees seek out birth family or birth family seek out adoptees, legal impediments have been put in the way of both parties by sealing birth records and making adoption files inaccessible. While there has been some progress made toward allowing for the exchange of identifying information between these parties, this is far from an automatic right. Most jurisdictions have put some form of veto on this process, allowing one of the parties either to keep the other from gaining access to identifying information or to impose a veto on any future contact between the parties. The paradox of this situation, of course, is that although restricted access to identifying information may keep adoptees and birth family apart, their mutual presence is made more salient by the absurd circumstance that adoptees are not automatically allowed to know their origins. If this is difficult to fathom, try a little experiment. Tell a few friends that you possess important information about their personal lives but that you are not at liberty to divulge the facts to them. See whether they simply walk away and seem unperturbed by this message. Of course, it will bother them and color every one of your future encounters. In the same way, sealed records do not protect the integrity of the adoptive family. Instead, they add one more stressor to adoptive family life by complicating the interactions between adoptees and their adopted parents. Hence, a strategy put into place to shore up the legitimacy of the adopted family, in fact, weakens it by continually pointing out its inability to deal with a history shared between two families.

Inaccessibility to an accurate and complete personal history also brings forth another form of structural discrimination against adoptees, their birth parents and other close birth relatives: They are denied a full medical history.

When adoptions are initially facilitated, a medical history is usually sought from the birth parents. Whether both birth parents are part of the process or whether they are able to give a complete family medical history will affect the accuracy of the file. In contested adoptions, where severance of legal ties is an acrimonious affair, it is likely that the birth relatives will not willingly participate in a fact-finding exercise with social workers charged with preparing a pre adoption record. And even if the file is complete at the time of placement, there is no guarantee that the medical history will reflect the medical status of the birth family twenty, thirty or forty years later. Many genetically mediated diseases do not appear until later in life. Having an initial history will not allow one to take preventive action if there is nothing in the record that would indicate that the adoptee is at future risk for displaying a genetically mediated disease. What is of equal importance and concern is that the future children of the adoptee are also at risk for not knowing the genetic status of their birth grandparents and extended birth kin. Disease may be passed from generation to generation, yet the law does not provide any mechanism for forewarning adoptees and their children of their genetic risk. In fact, the law does not even have a provision for informing adoptees that they have been adopted. While it is rare today to find an adoptee who has discovered, only later in life, that the people who raised him were not his genetic kin, there is no legal obligation to inform adoptees of this fact. Thus, the law treats adoptees and non-adoptees differentially. The latter group has access to biological kin and possesses accurate birth registration records. Adoptees, however, have no legal right to full, up-to-date information about their birth kin, and therefore, are always at genetic risk for being unable to access a complete medical history. Could there be a more blatant example of structural discrimination?

Placement without Access.

The demographics of adoption placement have shifted dramatically over the past two decades (Sobol & Daly, 1993). While infant placements were once the norm, today a majority of children who find their way to adoptive homes are above the age of four, have been in multiple foster homes and being older, may have spent considerable time with birth and foster families. For many of these children, the relationships that were formed prior to the adoption placement play a meaningful part in their young lives. The courts, in turn, have recognized the importance of these emotional ties by granting some birth families restricted access to their children. One must assume that such access serves the best interests of the child, for how else could it be justified? Therefore, it is difficult to understand the reasoning behind the fact that several jurisdictions will not allow adoption placements to occur if the child's protection order includes access provisions. This, in turn, has forced social workers to place these children quickly before access orders are put into effect. And of course, who suffers? The children.

Of all the parties to an adoption, children are in the least powerful position. Decisions are made about them. Rarely, is their input or consent sought. The law gives the state and the courts the right to determine whom the child will live with and whom the child is to call parent. While some jurisdictions will respect the child's right to reject an access order to someone from the child's past, the child is not granted the right, if desired, to maintain a meaningful relationship with those who have played a relational role in the child's upbringing.

Perhaps a common example will help to flesh out this issue. A cognitively limited young woman gives birth. She lacks the requisite functional skills to raise her child. Family and a wider network of support may be missing from her life. Recognizing that she is incapable of raising the child, social services remove the child to a foster setting and the parent is legally stripped of her parental rights. However, the court recognizes that the mother is a loving parent who is still very much connected to the child and therefore, grants access orders to the mother under supervised conditions. Time passes, and the decision is made to place the child for adoption. If the jurisdiction does not allow adoption placement with access orders, then steps are taken to remove the access orders, thus, freeing up the child for adoption. Following placement of the child in the adoptive home, the adoptive parents decide that in order for the child to feel that they are the "real" parents, they refuse to allow the birth mother to have any future contact with her child. This, of course, is their right under the law. However, what of the rights of the child, and of the birth mother, for that matter? The child has formed an important emotional relationship with the birth mother, even though it is recognized by all, including the child, that the birth mother is incapable of baring the full responsibilities of a parent. The birth mother will not simply disappear out of the psyche of the child just because the adoptive parents think that absence means eventual disappearance. The birth mother is an important reality in the emotional life of the child and paradoxically will take on even more importance to the extent that she is kept away from the child.

Often, one hears the argument that adoption placement without access to significant others in the child's life is the only means of protecting the child from those who might have been abusive in the past. No one would argue that a child should ever be put in such dangerous circumstances. However, it is hard to fathom how access orders could have been granted prior to adoption placement if such orders were thought to be a threat to the child in the future. Since there is no evidence that access orders are harmful to the child, we must look elsewhere for an explanation.

Perhaps the reasoning behind this practice is that access will prevent the child from forming meaningful relationships with the adoptive parents. Clearly, the "as if born to" clause in many adoption laws was included to stress the need for a "natural" or "real" connection between adoptees and their adoptive parents. Consanguineous parent-child relationships do not come with access orders except in the case of divorce or separation, and here the access is to a biological parent. Therefore, if adoptive parent-child relationships were to be accepted as the real thing, then the child's access to others would be seen as not supporting the fiction that the adoptive family is the same as the consanguineous one. Instead of recognizing that families can come in diverse configurations, the child is made to suffer by restricting access to others who are meaningful in her life. This is a heavy price to pay to protect the appearances of legitimacy.

Structural Discrimination against Adoptive Parents.

As previously discussed, many of the forms of discrimination against birth parents and adoptees were carried out in the service of attempting to enhance the legitimacy of the adoptive parents. Nevertheless, this does not mean that adoptive parents are exempt from structural discrimination.

The law is ambivalent about adoptive parents. On the one hand, restrictions were put in place in an attempt to transform the adoptive family into the "real" family. Access to information about the birth family was made difficult by sealing the original birth registration. The law stipulated that adoptive children were "as if born to" the adoptive parents. And yet, in many situations, the law neither supports adoptive parents, nor does it provide equal treatment of adoptive and non-adoptive parents.

From the moment that a couple decides to seek an adoption, they are placed in an inferior position relative to non-adoptive families. Nowhere in law are there standards that stipulate that a couple must meet a particular criterion before they are permitted to have a child. In adoption, nothing could be farther from the truth. Couples seeking to adopt must undergo an extensive screening to determine whether they are suitable as candidates for adoption. Motivations for adoption, family and fertility history, income, education, religion, age, criminal history, housing, family and social support, and finally, views about adoption are all part of the home study used to determine whether the couple will be placed into the pool of prospective applicants. I am not suggesting that this screening is not warranted. It is important that children, whose life histories place them outside of the norm, be raised in homes that will be empathetic and responsive to their needs. Yet, few adoptive applicants remember the home study in positive terms. Most found it to be a necessary humiliation that had to be endured if they were to become adoptive parents. I have often heard adoptive parents state that the selves they presented to the assessor were not their true selves. They were frightened to step outside of their perceptions of what they thought the social worker wanted to hear. When they felt diminished by the substance or tone of the inquiries, they stifled these feelings in order not to make a negative impression. They were on trial and they wanted to be judged worthy, even if the process reinforced the view that they were fertilely-challenged and hence, living outside of the wider cultural definition of a real family. It is intriguing to ask whether those not seeking to adopt would voluntarily put themselves through the same process in order to receive permission to conceive and bare a child. I would suspect this would have quite a dampening effect on the birth rate.

David Kirk (1964) recognized that adoptive parents are role handicapped from the beginning of the adoption process. They have few models to show them how to begin to raise an adoptive family. The examples found in the wider culture tend to verge toward the extremes, being either troubled or exemplary families. Adoptive families also have little in the way of preparation time, prior to the placement of the child. While most consanguineous families have a good idea when the infant will come into the world, the adoptive family rarely knows what the date of arrival will be. In fact, even when they are chosen as the adoptive parents of a specific child, there is no guarantee that the child will be placed with them. To make the matter even more stressful from the perspective of the adopting couple, there is no guarantee that a placement will be permanent as all jurisdictions have some waiting period after the placement when the birth parent may withdraw consent to the adoption. This period is important to birth parents and I am not suggesting that it be removed. It is necessary to give the birth parent an opportunity to reflect on the wisdom of the placement at a time when the emotions of birth and the post partum period are less intense. Yet it underscores the tentativeness and lack of legal assuries faced by the adopting couple.

In most jurisdictions today, parents are granted paid parental leave and the promise that their position will be available to them when they return to the marketplace. Typically, these benefits are split between maternal and parental benefits. In the former case, women are given financial support in order that they are able to recover from the birth experience itself and are available to parent the infant during the earliest stages of development[11]. These maternal benefits are not usually available to adopting parents for it is assumed that since they have not participated in a birth, there is no issue of recovery from gestation. However, the research literature would suggest otherwise.

A direct comparison of mothers who adopted an infant and mothers who gave birth and parented their infant has been undertaken by Gjerdingen and Froberg (1991). A quick reading of this paper would seem to indicate that adoptive mothers fare better than birth mothers following the arrival of the child. This, in fact, was the conclusion of one senior physician who gave evidence in Canadian court proceedings that led to differential support for consanguineous mothers and adoptive parents. However, a careful assessment of the findings yields a very different picture. True, the results of the study were that birth mothers had more physical and mental health symptoms than did adoptive mothers. On the other hand, these two groups displayed less social activity following the arrival of the child and less physical and emotional readiness to return to work than did a cohort of childless women. Furthermore, as the authors suggest, the adoptive cohort may not have been a representative sample of the population of adoptive mothers. This conclusion was based upon the fact that a smaller proportion of adoptive mothers completed the questionnaires than

---

11 If an infant is immediately placed for adoption, the birth mother is typically not eligible to receive parental leave benefits. It seems that the physical recovery from birthing is an experience that is reserved exclusively for those who will go on to parent the child. This leads immediately to the question of whether, in fact, maternal leave benefits have anything at all to do with recovery from the birthing process. If it truly were so, then both birth mothers and those women whose children were not placed would be eligible for the same maternal leave benefits. This is clearly not the case and is another example of structural discrimination against birth mothers.

did birth mothers or controls. The authors conclude that the lower response rate was probably the result of nonparticipating adoptive mothers being " . . . women who are tired, depressed or physically ill [who] would not be inclined to complete questionnaires . . . " The authors then go on to surmise that " . . . these results suggest that postpartum recovery often requires more than six weeks for **both** biological and adoptive mothers . . . If many of the needs of new birth mothers have been overlooked, the health concerns of new adoptive mothers have been almost totally ignored. Although the adoptive mothers in this study seemed to be in good general health, they showed some effects of new motherhood - fatigue, decreased activities and some reluctance to return to outside employment. Health care workers need to be aware of the full range of health risks faced by **both** adoptive and birth mothers in the postpartum period (p.33)."

Most adoptive parents today are not adopting healthy infants. Instead, a majority of children being placed are older, have special needs, or are international children (Sobol & Daly, 1993). Many of these children have faced serious developmental challenges that will not allow them to make an easy transition into adoptive homes. Verhulst, Althaus, and Versluis-Den Bieman (1990) found that one third of non-domestic children who were placed in adoptive homes had been previously exposed to risk factors including mal-nutrition, physical and sexual abuse, drugs and alcohol in utero, multiple placements, and lack of medical care and immunization. One third of the exposed group, or approximately ten percent of all international adoptees go on to display adverse developmental patterns. Since many of these children are quiet, if not lethargic at the time of placement, due to their weakened condition, it comes as a shock to adoptive parents when they begin displaying challenging characteristics quite soon after placement. Many of these parents are unprepared for this turn of events (Shapiro, Shapiro & Paret, 2001). Furthermore, while parents of children adopted internation-ally may be eager to form a close relationship with their children, many of the children are reticent to come close emotionally to the parents. Taken together, atypical development and emotional distance make for very stressful parent-child relationships.

Mainemer, Gilman and Ames (1998) found that parental stress is a function of the length of time that children have spent in an orphanage prior to placement. Comparing parents whose children were Canadian-born non adoptees, with children who had been in a Romanian orphanage either for less than four months or more than eight months, they found that the latter group had parents displaying the highest level of stress. Furthermore, level of stress was positively related to the level of behavioral disturbance the child displayed: the more the child presented symptoms of behavioral disorder, the greater the parents' level of stress.

Many special needs placements today are of children who have been prenatally exposed to drugs such as crack cocaine, alcohol and heroin. Most of these children will display developmental trajectories leading to significant behavioral disturbance. Adoptive parents of drug exposed children report that their stress level is highest during the first three to five months after placement, with a lessening of stress over the course of the following year (McCarty, Waterman, & Burge, 1999). Subsequent parental stress reactions were directly proportional to the degree of developmental impairment that the child displayed.

Another study, by McGlone, Santos, & Kazama (2002) examined the stress patterns of parents who had adopted children displaying asthma, hearing loss, language/speech delays, cognitive impairments, and motor delays. A third of the children scored above the clinical cut off on the Child Behavior Checklist, an instrument widely used to assess behavioral difficulties. Another 60% had elevated scores on either the Internalizing or Externalizing scales. Clearly, this was a challenging group of children. And how did their adoptive parents fare? McGlone et al. found that the parents, not surprisingly had markedly elevated levels of stress and these stress levels did not diminish over the first year following placement.

In light of these findings, it is difficult to argue that adoptive parents are less entitled to post placement benefits than are consanguineous parents entitled to post partum benefits. Clearly, the needs of the two groups are different by virtue of the route that has led them to family formation. Nevertheless, there are no clinical grounds on which adoptive families are less entitled to equal treatment under the law. In fact, not to do so, regardless of the restriction in access to equal benefits, is, in itself an act of slighting the legitimacy of adoptive families. Openly discriminating against them by providing a lower level of benefits sends a strong public message concerning the fictive nature of this family form, and does little to strengthen their ability to build strong family relationships.

Perhaps the reluctance of most governments to provide equal benefits to adoptive and consanguineous families is more political than it first appears. To do so would open up a challenge from consanguineous fathers to receive the same benefits as adoptive parents in that neither group has need of physical recovery from the birth experience, as do consanguineous mothers. To accommodate this issue, I am not arguing that consanguineous mothers should lose maternal benefits. What is needed is a consideration of benefits for adoptive parents that is distinct from maternal benefits. This would recognize that there are needs in the adoptive family that are different from those in the consanguineous family. At the same time, these needs should be considered to be equally legitimate.

For those who wish to argue that adoptive parents are seeking a free ride, it should be noted that many jurisdictions require that one of the adoptive parents must not engage in outside employment during the early days of the placement, even if the child is older and attending school full time. Paradoxically, this requirement is imposed at the same time as these jurisdictions fail to support the adoptive family with an equivalent level of benefits as are given to non adoptive families. The reasoning behind this inconsistency remains an enigma.

A final example of structural discrimination toward adoptive families is the differential treatment they receive regarding citizenship and immigration. When a child is born to a Canadian national who is residing outside of the country, the child is automatically granted Canadian citizenship. However, if a child is adopted by a Canadian citizen outside of the country, the child does not enter Canada as a Canadian citizen but as an immigrant who eventually will be granted citizenship. It has been suggested that this disparity in the law prevents casual adoption, particularly of extended family, strictly for the purpose of bypassing current immigration laws. While this might be the case, such restrictions again send a message to adoptive families and to the wider community, that adopted children and their families are less real and less deserving of the full benefits of citizenship than are their non adopted counterparts.

A Political Response to Structural Discrimination

Clearly, these many examples of structural discrimination against birth parents, adoptees and adoptive parents describe a cultural pattern of diminishment of those in the inner orbits of the adoption constellation. Law, government policies and practitioner practices all attenuate the range of options open to adoptees and their birth and adoptive families. This is not surprising, given that those whose lives fall under the umbrella of adoption are playing out a family drama that is considered to be fictive, even though adoption serves the dual societal roles of providing homes for children, and children for infertile adults. Nevertheless, the culturally fictive label provides all the justification necessary to structurally discriminate against this family form on a societal level. How then should the adoption community respond to this situation?

At this time, the definition of a "real" family as genetically related kin has been so strongly ingrained in the cultural fabric of our society that it is hard to imagine making headway against such a view, particularly when there does not seem to be much motivation to do so.

Within the adoption constellation, there is a mixed response to changing this definition of family. Adoptive parents are uncomfortable with it as it will always place them outside of the normative discussion of family legitimacy, regardless of how successful they may be fulfilling family-related roles. That being said, for many adoptive parents, this definition is the only one to which they aspire: to be parents whose adopted children were as if born to them. It is for this reason that there has been little response from adoptive parents to change prevailing attitudes and practices in adoption, except in response to legislation that personally discriminates against them. A perusal of the web sites of such parent organizations as the Adoption Council of Canada and the North American Council on Adoptable Children reinforces this point. These are the two largest North American adoption organizations. Their issues of concern center around placement. Neither one of them has an articulated agenda and action plan for adoption advocacy beyond facilitation, or for post adoption support for adoptive families. It is not hard to find adoptive parent advocates who speak out against stigmatizing language that equates adoption of their children with the "adopting of a mile of highway" or an "animal from the pound." However, concern for access to information, the maintenance of openness agreements, contact between birth siblings, long term counseling for birth parents and the like, are simply off their radar screens.

In a similar fashion, birth parent and adoptee organizations have put their energies into open records and the psychological aftermath of placement and secrecy. One rarely hears concern expressed for those children who remain in interminable foster care without any hope of growing up in a setting of consistency and care.

In other words, there seems to be no political agenda for the complete constellation of adoption. Each element functions within its own orbit with little concern or respect for the other parts of the constellation. And what is the consequence of such splintered self-interest? Nothing changes. Legislators feel no need to amend discriminatory laws as little pressure is brought to bear from across the constellation. When open records are the issue at hand, adoptive parents do not step up to state unequivocally that access to a full history is in the best interests of their children. When attempts are made to find homes for children whose consanguineous families have forfeited their legal rights to parent through abuse, the adoptee and birth family communities say little at all to support adoption placements for these children. The consequence of this narrowed self-interest is the status quo.

If we are ever to see a lessening of stigma and its resulting discrimination in adoption, there must be recognition that a change in any aspect of adoption affects all elements within the constellation. Lessening stigma in one orbit creates a new context in which to perceive other parts of adoption. Until this principle of interrelationship between elements of the constellation is accepted, the power of the whole to bring about legislative reform will remain forever weak. Unless there is support for the agenda of the other, legislators will play one group off against the other and discrimination will remain embedded within the law. The choice of supporting others in the constellation is ours to make.

CHAPTER 4

A NARRATIVE UNDERSTANDING OF ADOPTIVE EXPERIENCE

I must pursue this trail to the end, till I have unraveled the mystery of my birth (Oedipus in Sophocles' Oedipus Rex)

The adoptive uncle of a five-year-old boy told me the following story:

My nephew Jered came into our family at the age of three weeks. He had been born in central British Columbia in the city of Kamloops, to a young woman whose life circumstances led her to adoption. Two years later, Jered's parents again began the process of adopting another child. When Jered was four, they received news that there was an infant available for adoption at the same agency from which they had adopted Jered. And so, off they went, leaving Jered in the care of my very pregnant wife and me. During our second day together, Jered noticed the rounded shape of my wife and asked why she was so large. Seeing this as a potential learning opportunity, she asked him if he knew where babies came from, to which Jered replied most proudly "Of course I know where babies come from. They come from Kamloops!!

To this young lad, the beginnings of his adoption narrative seemed so simple and straightforward. None of the cultural stigmata associated with adoption as a fictive family form were apparent in his understanding of adoption. He had a few facts at hand, and the cognitive competence to shape an elementary story of adoptive family formation. His arrival in the family, and the impending arrival of his new adoptive sibling did not seem out of the ordinary. For Jered, one simply went to Kamloops and found a new brother. From his perspective and level of development, what more was there to say?

Of all the things that characterize adoption, the creation of narrative perhaps plays the most pre-eminent role. Adoptive parents offer renditions of their journeys from infertility to adoptive parenthood. Birth parents are challenged to find a storied theme to describe their lives without the physical presence of children whom they had brought into the world. For many without contact with their children, this means that their life story has the feel of one that has ended at the conclusion of chapter one, the placement of the child. In parallel manner, adoptees are faced with fashioning a narrative that for many, excludes the first chapter of their lives.

Individuals construct past events and actions in personal narratives in order to claim particular kinds of identities and to construct an understanding of specific life courses (Rosenwald & Ochberg, 1992). In telling stories, we emphasize some things and omit others. We take particular stances as active protagonists or victims. We use our story line not only to describe relationships between ourselves and those who touch us emotionally but also to establish a relationship between ourselves as narrators and our audiences. Personal stories aid us in establishing common ground with others. We draw upon our stories to elicit social support. If our self-stories are out of sync with those around us, we quickly find ourselves under the influence of revisionist attempts to reshape them to fall in line with current, dominant narratives (Gergen, 1985).

However, not all stories are for public consumption. Some of our narrative work is only accessible to the self. We have stories that we share with others, and we have stories that are reserved for our inner selves alone. These latter narratives may differ in tone, structure or content from our public narratives.

Private narratives can serve as a dress rehearsal for public narratives which might be used in the future. They are means for exploring alternatives through the consideration of different plot lines in which we strive to make sense of our past, account for our present and lay the ground work for future action. In our private narratives, we can take chances without major social consequences. Imaging our selves projected along different plot lines, we are able to experiment with newly emerging themes in our lives. All of these activities can better prepare us as we move from private to public renditions of our narratives.

However, when our internal stories are negatively shaded and our external stories reflect a more positive tone, feelings of discontinuity and inauthenticity may result. The brave face of the public narrator may be forced by social pressure to conform to a particular standard of what is expected to be heard by others. The narrator may wrongly perceive the expectations of the audience or fear the consequences of violating the norms of acceptable narrative production, even when the audience has no intention of socially condemning a discordant narrative. In such circumstances, narrators are left feeling that they are hiding their true selves. In such circumstance, stories are told, not to authenticate the self by reflecting private narratives but only to hold the audience. This discordant bifurcation of the private and the public is most apparent when one has experienced a loss and its accompanying grief but the audience does not wish to know the details of the private narrative. This should sound familiar to those whose lives are bound up in adoption and will be a theme that will be explored further.

Narrative and Identity

Personal stories utilize the self as the central character in the plot line. Thus, individuals become the autobiographical narratives that they tell to themselves and to others. In this sense, we are our own stories.

At the heart of self-as-protagonist is the notion of a core of sameness in the face of growth and change. Thus, I am the same person in spite of my white beard and balding head as I was as a pimply-faced adolescent. Physical characteristics may have altered, emotions may have moderated, however, the sense of "me" continues unabated. In other words, we have an identity or "sense of personal sameness and historical continuity" (Erikson, 1968, p.17).

While not necessarily explicitly presented in our narratives, our sense of self is influenced to some degree by our perception of how others recognize in us both sameness and continuity (Erikson, 1968). When our transitions across development occur in an orderly and smooth fashion, others will have little difficulty seeing us as possessing a consistent and continuous identity. However, when transitions are marked by conflict, discord and antagonism, it is common to receive feedback from significant others that alters our sense of self in the direction of a storied theme that accounts for seeming discontinuities. How individuals utilize others' identity messages will contribute to a sense of selfhood. Mead (1934) referred to this phenomenon as "reflected appraisal," the sense of self based on the perceptions of others' appraisal of us.

However, identity, imbedded in a life narrative, is not just the result of the acceptance of social direction offered by others in our immediate social milieu. There are also wider forces at play here. At the societal level, overriding definitions of selfhood are grounded in such factors as gender role expectations, ethnic membership, and citizenship. Few individuals are able to develop a rendition of self-in-time that is outside of the boundaries provided by these societal parameters. To the extent that a person occupies positions of minority status or has been stigmatized within the wider culture, the more salient and restricting will be the definitions of self. Clearly, this should have important implications for what it means to be a member of the inner rings of the adoption constellation.

Yet, in framing a sense of self in narrative time, we are not hapless recipients of externally imposed considerations. Each of us, to a greater or lesser extent, engages in internal structuring of our stories of self. Composition of a narrative is moderated by two factors in addition to membership in one's culture and the pressures of social interaction.

These are one's underlying personality structure (Oliver & Srivastava, 1999)[12] and temperament, which have a substantial genetic component and are decontextualized in that there is a fair degree of consistency in thought and action across settings. In addition, attitudes, goals and expectations, which Wilson (2002) refers to as the "adaptive unconscious" plays a part in shaping the narrative. These latter factors are grounded in experience and have a context-specific influence on narrative construction. As an act of personal agency, we attend, sort and organize information into a coherent narrative structure.

This structure sustains a historical sense of self. Our identity stories are, thus, imbued with "the capacity to integrate the individual's reconstructed past, perceived present, and anticipated future, rendering a life-in-time sensible in terms of beginnings, middles, and endings (McAdams, 1996, p. 307)." By casting ourselves into narrative time, we provide meaning as to how we change over the course of our lives. We offer motivations and causal explanations embedded within our stories to account for why we have acted as we have. We try to make our stories appear to follow a rational course. When the stories of our lives appear incomplete, we fill the gaps with strong emotions that cover over the missing parts. Our stories are designed to give meaning to whom we have been, who we are, and who we will be in the future and as such, provide integration of the self over the passage of time (Riessman,1993).

Development of an adoption narrative

The course of narrative development follows three broadly defined stages (McAdams, 1996). In the first or prenarrative era, infants, children and young adolescents compile experiences that will later be incorporated into their articulated life stories. The narrative era marks the second stage and begins at the point in development when the individual begins to construct a "self-defining life story."

12 Researchers in personality theory has identified five broad traits that seem to express universal dimensions of personality. They are extraversion, agreeableness, conscientiousness, neuroticism, and openness to experience.

This era typically starts in late adolescence or early adulthood and continues throughout adulthood as the individual redefines and reshapes an identity of self, grounded in a personal narrative. In the final stage, referred to as the post narrative era, the narrator has reached a point in life where the end is clearly in sight. There is little refashioning of narrative at this point. Instead, life stories are recounted and assessed in an attempt to determine whether they will be personally accepted, allowing for a sense of integrity, or rejected with its accompanying sense of despair (Erikson, 1963).

Prenarrative Era.

As outlined in Chapter 2, there is a stream of adoption-related theorizing that would argue that the defining moments in narrative development are to be found in utero in the months leading up to the point of forced separation between mother and infant. This is clearly a period within the prenarrative era of narrative production. Having been intertwined in a symbiotic relationship for nine months, the birthmother and fetus have learned to dance to the biorhythms of the other. Eldridge (2003, p. 50-51), based on the writings of Verny (1981) and Janov (1991) describes an interchange between fetus and mother as follows:

> "If we [adoptees] heard, 'I love you and am so glad you're a part of me. I will do all that I can to help you develop into the person you were created to be. I can't wait to see you. I will welcome you into the world in a way more wonderful than you can imagine,' our [the adoptee's] response was certainly positive. We would have thrived on it. 'Oh, Mommy,' our little preverbal minds might have said, 'I love you so much and I can't wait to be born so that I can suckle at your breasts and be held in your arms.'
>
> On the other hand, what if we heard, 'I don't want you. I don't even like you. In fact, I think of you as an 'it' and frankly, I can't wait to get rid of you. I wish I could.'

Our little minds may have responded like this: 'All alone. All alone. Hurts so bad. No one will ever take care of me. I must 'buck up' and be strong so I can survive. Be strong. Be strong. Tense up. Be on guard so I won't be tortured like this again.'"

For many of the prenatal theorists, this vignette is a literary account of a nonverbal dialogue between mother and fetus. They believe that it reflects an unarticulated sense of joy or dread that accompanies the fetus through to the end of gestation. And then, in one sudden and heart wrenching instant, the fetus is thrust down the birth canal and birthmother and her child are ripped apart. Each is said to carry the psychic scars of this forced separation until such time as they are reunited, and even then, the psychic scar tissue of this harsh early separation may still fester. For the infant, lacking sophisticated cognitive skills to symbolically code these intense feelings, the experience of these events will be stored in memory as unarticulated, disconnected emotions of pain, loss, anger and depression. These early emotions will tone all subsequent relationships in terms of lowered expectations of others, an inability to connect and be intimate, a sense of powerlessness and a feeling that one is not entitled to belong to either the adoptive family or any relationships extending beyond these familial boundaries.

Such theoretical speculation has won wide acceptance within the adoptee and birthparent communities, despite the fact that there is very little evidence from the early developmental research literature to support such a perspective. So why does such theorizing receive such wide public support? I believe it is because writers like Verrier (1991) and Eldridge (2003) have been able to successfully capture and describe the existential sense of loss and its accompanying pain that many adoptees experience. These are some of the most salient and emotionally tinged elements of many adoption narratives. However, accurate description does not necessarily imply that the explanation offered for these emotional elements of the adoption narrative is veridical. Given the lack of support for this popular explanatory account of these very real emotions, let us turn to an alternative explanation, centered on the narrative rendering of separation, loss, and placement within an adoptive family.

In utero and infant experience. The prenarrative era begins in utero with the experience of cyclical moments of excitation and inhibition of arousal. These are changes in physiological levels away from and back to a level of adaptation. These are not emotions as we normally think of them, for emotions require excitation as well as the cognitive appraisal and symbolic labeling of the meaning of the excitation (Schachter and Singer, 1962).

The fetus lacks the capacity to engage in these higher cognitive functions of providing meaningful labels for physiological excitation. This function will only appear when the child has developed enough symbolic thinking to be able to cognitively assess and label unspecified excitation by providing a contextual meaning. Thus, emotional experiences at this period are confined to background increases and decreases in excitation. If the stimuli that precede these moments of excitatory experience occur in regular fashion so that they are predictable, and if the periods of excitation are not so prolonged as to become overly aversive, then infants will have the opportunity to learn the patterning of this excitation. With time, they will develop strategies to maintain excitation within comfortable bounds. The end result of this process is the structuring of emotional responding with its accompanying future cognitive appraisal and emotional labeling. It serves as the precursor to a sense of predictability and contributes to a growing feeling of control over one's internal experience. None of this is clearly articulated nor is the infant personally cognizant of a range of emotions at an early period, but it does set the tone for the future of emotional experience and hence, adds to the emotional valence of the emerging narrative.

Early experience for infant and caretaker primarily centers around meeting the infant's survival needs for food, warmth and physical security. The contexts in which this takes place include feeding, bathing, holding, and playful interactions. Each situation provides an opportunity for an encounter between the caretaker and the infant in which each participant shapes and modifies the behavior of the other.

In the most general sense, this period is one in which the infant needs to maintain a sense of homeostasis, a balance between extremes. When the infant experiences excitation in the form of signals that homeostasis is not operative, she will send out distress signals to the caretaker indicating that there is a need to take action. The infant might display rooting behavior in an attempt to find the breast if hungry, or cry out in pain if intense stimulation such as a loud noise or skin irritation is present. The caretaker's task is to find a means of lessening the distressing stimulation, thus allowing the infant to return to a state of quiescence. If the caretaker is responsive to the infant and if the infant experiences the caretaker as a source of lessening intense stimulation, then when in a state of distress, the infant will seek out the caretaker. Repeated patterning of excitation and quiescence sets the stage for what emerges as an attachment relationship. If the caretaker is experienced as a source of relief from discomfort, then the growing infant is more likely to reach out beyond the boundaries of the relationship in order to explore the wider environs of her world. This inevitably results in increased arousal, an uncomfortable state, and a return of the infant to the proximity of the caretaker where each finds comfort in the close presence of the other. This serves as the early basis for feelings of trust and security in close, intimate relationships. Such interaction between caretaker and infant is an example of a secure attachment relationship.

However, this excitation-quiescence cycle is not the one that all infants and their caretakers experience. For some infants, they quickly learn that caretakers are not a source of relief from uncomfortable stimulation. This can happen for many reasons. The caretaker may be unaware of when the infant is experiencing highly uncomfortable levels of stimulation or may be aware of the fact, but lacks the skills or resources to lower the infant's level of excitation. If this is the case, then the infant may remain in close proximity to the caretaker but will display intense distress reactions directed toward the caretaker's attempts at meeting the infant's needs. This describes ambivalent attachment. Another possibility is that when confronted with such stimulation, the infant will simply not look to the caretaker for relief. This is particularly apparent when not only does the caretaker fail to lessen discomfort but actually increases the distress level of the infant by providing addition excitatory stimulation in the form of yelling, pushing the infant away or physical abuse. The inevitable result is that the infant learns that close contact with the caretaker is not a source of comforting and hence, the infant disengages from the adult. Sadly, the caretaker in such circumstances may label the infant's withdrawal as a hostile maneuver and may respond with even more intense acts of rejecting. This form of relationship is referred to as avoidant attachment.

A final form of attachment is disorganized attachment. Here, the infant has had a very mixed encounter with the caretaker. At times, the caretaker is an effective reducer of aversive stimulation. At other times, the caretaker is a source of such stimulation. The result is that the infant does not know whether to seek out or avoid the caretaker. There will be occasions when approaching the caretaker for relief of distress will be met with effective parenting but there will also be episodes when approaching the caretaker will result in a hostile response to the infant. The consequence of this inconsistency is that the infant will likely display disorganized attachment in which there is no consistent pattern of seeking out relief after exposure to overstimulation.

A cursory reading of these scenarios would easily lead one to assume that infant attachment style is in the hands of the caretaker. Warm, responsive and consistent management of the infant's excitatory experience leads to secure attachment but inept, rejecting or inconsistent care taking will result in distressed attachment patterns. Such a linear view of attachment ignores that fact that the excitation-quiescence cycle is, in reality, a dance between partners. The caretaker is not the only one leading. The infant also plays a significant, active role. Some infants have a gentle temperament that makes the task of comforting them quite easy, even for the most inexperienced and anxious caretaker. Other infants, are born with a temperamental style that would challenge even the most resourceful and effective caretaker's ability to lower excitation. These individual differences in temperamental style are primarily genetic in origin (Kagan, 1994). The closer the genetic connection of infant and biological relative, the more similar will be their temperamental style. Thus, it is birthparents and not adoptive parents who determine the child's early temperament. For the most part, easy-going birthparents give birth to easy-going infants. Emotionally labile birthparents will likely bring infants into the world who will have difficulty maintaining an even keel.

However, this is not to say that environmental factors, both physical and emotional, do not also play a part. Sadly, thousands of children who have been exposed to excessive amounts of alcohol during gestation have gone on to develop a cluster of neuropsychological symptoms referred to as Fetal Alcohol Syndrome. FAS is characterized by distortions in physiognomy, inattentiveness, emotional labiality including difficulty in controlling anger and physical aggression and a myriad of learning disabilities (Streissguth, Barr, Bookstein, Sampson & Olson, 1999). As infants, FAS children are generally difficult to comfort, irritable and excitable. Other environmental factors have also been identified as putting the infant at risk for future development. These include poor maternal nutrition during gestation, lack of medical scrutiny of the pregnancy, poor postnatal nutrition, multiple caretakers and placement settings, institutional rearing, and abusive caretakers (Verhulst, Althaus, and Versluis-den Bieman, 1990,1992).

Verrier (1992) has argued that only the consanguineous mother can successfully serve as the primary care taker of her infant. She is the only one who has any chance of forming a secure attachment relationship as she is the only one who has shared biorhythms with her child. Together they have formed an attachment that is established well before the birth. It is she that the infant recognizes and it is her emotional life that the fetus, and then infant, will mirror. However, if the consanguineous relationship is the only foundation for a secure attachment, then we must be able to address two issues. The first pertains to whether adoptive parent-child attachment relationships differ from consanguineous relationships. This question was previously addressed. Substituting an adoptive parent for a consanguineous parent has seemingly no effect on the infant's attachment relationship with the caretaker parent. There is no difference in the proportion of each attachment style found in consanguineous and adoptive relationships (Brodzinsky et al, 1983). The second point to remember is that consanguinity is no guarantee of secure attachment relationships. In non-adoptive families, at least half of all attachment relationships are not categorized as secure. Being the genetic infant of the caretaker does not insure that the infant will feel comfort and security in the presence of the caretaker. As Goldstein, Freud and Solnit (1979, p.17) have stated: "...for the child, the physical realities of his conception and birth are not the direct cause of his emotional attachment. This attachment results from the day-to-day attention to his needs for physical care, nourishment, comfort, affection and stimulation." It would seem that it is not so much with whom one is dancing that is important, but how well each dancer can interact with the other. Skilful and relaxed parents and temperamentally easy infants will be the most successful partners. All others will struggle to find a comfortable rhythm together.

Let us consider how these factors relate to adoptive narrative identity? Attachment relationships and the attendant experiences of early life, such as feeding, being held, bathing, and play, are said to serve as the developmental precursors for many characteristics: the emergence of interpersonal trust and a sense of security; comfort with close relationships and intimacy; self-efficacy; self-esteem; and joyfulness. There is evidence to suggest that those who were securely attached as infants will as adults, feel comfortable in close, intimate relationships, will see the past with a sense of clarity and will display positive affect for the past. Avoidant infants are said to develop into adults who tend to minimize the importance of interpersonal connections. Adults with a past, marked by ambivalent attachments, are found to overly focus on relationships, to display anger and helplessness and are not satisfied with the current level of closeness in their relationships. Finally, those adults who experienced disorganized attachment as infants, seem cognitively and emotionally disoriented in their adult relationships. They have trouble making sense of interpersonal cues and motivations. They may feel helpless and take on the identity of the victim or are hostile and interpersonally aggressive (Cassidy & Shaver, 1999).

This description of the developmental route from infant attachment relationships to adult intimate relationships would seem to encompass the range of experiences of adult adoptees. Those who have had secure infant attachments would be expected to be comfortable with their past, and feel that their current relationships meet their needs. Avoidantly attached adoptees, as adults, would show little interest in their origins, would be less motivated to re-establish connection with birth family and would not feel particularly close to adoptive relatives. Adult adoptees who were classified as ambivalently attached as young children would be expected to display intense interest in birth origins, be dissatisfied with the degree of closeness in their adoptive family, and would feel incapable or making their adult relationships work. Finally, they would be expected to feel the least satisfaction with the degree of closeness experienced in their intimate relationships. As for those adults classified as having experienced early disorganized attachment, the expectation would be that they either would feel very much the victim of their early life experiences or would push others away through the display of anger and aggression.

These predictions follow directly from the wider literature on early attachment and later adult relationships, and would seem to account for the range of adult adoptee experiences. They suggest that early experience sets the stage for later development. It is assumed that knowing the beginning of a developmental trajectory will confidently permit predictions with regard to what the person will be like as an adult. This is an example of what Lewis (1997) referred to as a linear model of development. Once started in a direction, the person is destined to continue along that route determined in early experience. Unfortunately, life is rarely as simple as proponents of linear models of development have suggested. Yes, there is some relationship between early experience and later development. However, the relationship is not a strong one and in most cases similar beginnings result in multiple outcomes. So what accounts for the weak relationship between past and future?

Lewis (1997) has suggested that the answer lies in the social and physical context in which development occurs. When there are structures in place that continue to support a particular developmental trajectory over time, then the context serves as a bridge between past and future. For example, if a parent is warm and supportive early in the infant's life and continues to act in a similar manner throughout the early life of the child, then the secure attachment in infancy should be related to later secure relationships. An adopted child with such a history comes to understand that one can trust those who are close to him. However, if early secure attachment is followed by a dramatic change in the context of development, then early models of relationships will no longer hold. For example, when a parent is prone to cyclical bouts of depression, then an earlier secure attachment style will not continue into later life as the parent is not able to sustain a secure relationship with her child over time. An early secure attachment in such circumstances might result in a later sense of ambiguity, avoidance or disorganization, depending on the nature of the post-infancy experience with a now dysfunctional parent. In other words, development is linear only to the extent that later developmental contexts are consistent with previous experience. Otherwise, development follows discontinuous trajectories. The child brings with him adaptive strategies from previous encounters. However, they will be utilized only to the extent that they match the developmental demands of the current context.

Thus, knowing one's early beginnings will tell us less about development than will an analysis of the demands of the child's developmental context. For adoptees, one of the most important aspects of the developmental context is the manner in which adoption-related issues are managed in the family and beyond. It is here that the child, and later the adolescent, gathers the facts that will be incorporated into a narrative of adoption identity and ultimately, personhood.

Early Telling of the Adoption Story.
The events leading up to an adoption are potential materials for the adoptee's adoption narrative. These include the route that was taken from birth family to adoptive family and the subsequent assimilation of the child into the adoptive family. However, these events remain background factors, shading emotional relationships in the adoptive family. It is only when the adoptive parent introduces the child to the idea of being adopted that these events take on potential psychological significance as facts for a future adoption identity, embedded within a wider life narrative.

Many adoptive parents dread the first telling of the adoption story for it brings to an end the fantasy that this, indeed, is their "real" child who belongs to them and to no other. They often fear the potential emotional reaction of the child to the idea of being adopted and the possibility of sending the child down a path of dual loyalty to birth and adoptive families.

On the other hand, most children who are told a rudimentary version of their adoption story at a young age are not disturbed by the first telling. Like Jered, quoted at the beginning of this chapter, adoption has little early significance. Lacking the cognitive sophistication to understand the full import of being adopted, the first telling seems natural to most young adoptees. Some children are curious how one can move from family to family. Others simply accept the fact that they have taken this journey, seeing nothing in it that is exceptional or of particular concern.

There was a time in adoptive practice when it was recommended that adoptive parents wait at least until the child was seven years of age before telling the child of the adoption. This age was chosen as it was believed that an earlier telling would interfere with the child's ability to identify with the same-sex adoptive parent. Such psychoanalytic guidance has not proven to be valid as there is no evidence that early telling of the adoption story in any way interferes with psychosexual development. In fact, the early telling can be beneficial, not just for the child, but also for the parents. If the parent begins to speak of adoption well before the young child is able to fully understand the implications of the story, the parent will gain practice and confidence in the oration. By choosing an early telling, there is little room to let secrecy and all of its restrictions enter into the relationship. There is no need to distort relations in the service of maintaining a fabricated rendition. When adoption is a normalized concept that is part of the lexicon of the family, then less will be invested emotionally by parents when telling the story. Given that emotional tone at an early age is as important as the actual details, early practice prepares the parent for a time in the future when a retelling of the journey to adoption will carry with it stronger feelings about loss and grief.

Watkins and Fisher (1993) have suggested that the first loss experienced by adoptees may take place at that point in the child's early development when there is some rudimentary understanding of the origin of babies. The child comes to learn that the adoptive mother, the parent who has formed an attachment with the child through a myriad of acts of nurturing, is not the source of the child's origin. Knowledge of this fact may be experienced by the child as a loss of opportunity for early connection with the adoptive mother. This is expressed as a protest against being carried during pregnancy by another person and may be felt as a threat to the attachment that has been formed between the child and a caring adoptive parent. This is truly paradoxical for it is not the loss of the birth mother but the loss of an early connection with the adoptive mother that may prove to be the first experience of early pain in the telling of the adoption story. And it is not just the child who will experience the pain of loss. For most adoptive parents, there also is a sense of loss at not having had the opportunity to experience the act of carrying the child through gestation. Many adoptees, particularly those born in the early 1980's report being told at a very young age that "Mommy didn't carry you under her heart. She carried you in her heart." The intent of the message is that the adoptive mother is expressing her strong connection to the child. The more subtle message is that her emotional relationship takes precedence over the birth mother's genetic connection. While this message may be motivated by the adoptive parent's desire to assuage the child's sense of loss, it also sets up a challenge to any feelings of dual loyalty that the child might have. That being said, this parallel sense of loss, experienced by adoptive mother and adoptee, does provide a unique opportunity for the mutual sharing of feelings. If this occurs in a respectful and developmentally sensitive manner, it may contribute to a strengthening of the interconnectedness of adoptive parent and child.

If, however, the style of early attachment between parent and child does not flow naturally from mutual interactions that take place in a nurturing context, then this telling of the pregnancy story likely will be experienced by the child as a further threat to a sense of security within the parent-child relationship. In this case, the child, before the telling, did not feel securely connected to the parent. Now the child carries the additional burden of sensing that another woman also felt disconnected enough from the child that she did not sustain a continuing relationship following the pregnancy. Most adoptive parents try to counter this interpretation of the events leading to the adoption by assuring the child that the birth parent loved but could not care for the child and so the adoptive parents came to adopt the child. Nevertheless, the child in such circumstances is left with a feeling of loss of the first caretaker, the birth parent. What the child does with these feelings is very much a result of the subsequent stages of the telling of the adoption story.

The Possible Impermanence of Connection.

Up until the age of six, few children, regardless of adoptive status, are able to differentiate between adoption and birth as separate processes for becoming part of a family. (Brodzinsky, Singer and Braff, 1984). The idea of having two sets of parents, one of which was responsible for the birth and the other responsible for current parenting is simply missing from the child's understanding. This would suggest that the early telling of the adoption story has relatively little impact on the adopted child's notions of how he came into the adoptive family. However, by the age of seven, most children view adoption and birth as two distinct routes for joining a family. These children may not be absolutely certain as to the meaning of these concepts. Nevertheless, they are aware that they represent alternative processes of family formation. More importantly, children at this age believe that the relationship between the child and the adoptive parents is absolute and unbreakable. As one of Brodzinsky et al's participants reported, "It's their baby now . . . no one can take it" (p.872). It is, therefore, not surprising that most children of this age are not disturbed by the knowledge that they have been adopted. They are too young to have picked up the cultural stigma attached to adoption and are not threatened by an uncertain future with their adoptive parents.

Such relative tranquility, however, is not long lasting. Somewhere between the ages of eight and eleven, there is a major shift in the child's thinking about permanence in adoption. At this point, children come to recognize that the original entrance into the birth family was not marked by a permanent connection between themselves and their family of origin. If they could be removed from their first family, then why could they not also be removed from their adoptive family? Thus, family relationships become tenuous as the child explores the idea of reversibility of relationships and entertains fantasies about being reclaimed by the birth parents. As one child put it, " . . . I think his real parents might get him back if they wanted him" (Brodzinsky et al., p.872).

There are major consequences for this advance in the cognitive appreciation of what adoption is all about. The adopted child, having gained an understanding of impermanence, now comes to appreciate more fully what it means to be "relinquished." Questions will come to mind about the birth parents' appraisal of the worth of the child and whether he represented enough value to have been kept by them. For many adoptees struggling with this issue, the assurance of the adoptive parents that "the birth mother loved you so much that she chose to give you a better life" is hardly of much comfort. However, the reality for adoptees is that they were "given up." When the birth parent is not there to tell her story in person, when the adoptive parents possess only a rudimentary rendition of these events, devoid of facts and an appreciation of the context in which decisions were made around placement, then adoptees are often left with little choice other than to draw such a conclusion and to devalue their self worth.

The facts, as understood by the adoptee, are concrete and convincing: one family did not keep them; and another family, usually without consanguineous children, took up the option of being substitute parents to a rejected child. Is it any wonder then, that during middle childhood we begin to see an increase in emotional indices of distress in adopted children (Brodzinsky et al., 1992)? Their understanding of adoption is fraught with contradictions and challenges. They must determine whether one or both sets of parents are real and legitimate. A decision must be made as to whether they will accept early attachment to adoptive parents as the definition of parenthood or will incorporate the cultural definition of biological kinship as the only true definition of family (Leon, 2002). They are forced to address the conflict between a fantasy about a return to birth family and the early attachment to adoptive parents. And as if the situation was not complicated enough, the preteen must also deal with the possibility of being rejected by the adoptive parents. In the child's mind, if birth parents were willing to let the adoption occur, then is it not also possible that the adoptive parents might reject the child in the future?

Brodzinsky et al. (1984) also noted two other shifts in the developmental understanding of what adoption means to the child. By the age of eleven, most adopted children recognize that permanency is a legal reality, in that they are tied to adopted parents by the force of law. The parameters of this legal tie, however, cannot yet be articulated by the child. By early adolescence, this changes somewhat. The young adopted teen now recognizes the difference between legal and psychological ties and will be aware that these two connections do not always work in parallel. These children are aware that their relationship with adopted parents is a legal reality that cannot easily be torn asunder. At the same time, their psychological connection to the adoptive parents is open to a range of possibilities. For some, there is a feeling of acceptance and emotional closeness. For others, the legal ties are recognized as holding the family together, yet there is the feeling of great emotional distance between themselves and the other constituent members of the family.

Identity formation and adoptive identity.

As adoptees enter adolescence, they like all adolescents, face the challenge of establishing a cohesive definition of the self (Erikson,1968). This definition of self is both global and specific. In the former sense, the task is one of painting a personal picture in broad cultural strokes of gender, class, and ethnicity. In the more restricted sense of specific identity, adolescents are faced with describing what it is that makes them who they are as distinct individuals. For adolescents who have been adopted, this can be a formidable challenge. Specifically, they need to incorporate into an integrated sense of self such factors as an evaluation of their intellectual, social, emotional, occupational and recreational selves. In addition, they must deal with the cultural, familial, and personal definitions of adoption that mark them as different from the norm (Grotevant, 1997, 2000). As if the situation is not complex enough, adopted adolescents must also achieve some balance between the prominence they will give to adoption as a defining characteristic of self and other life-course experiences set outside of adoption, per se.

Identity has been construed by Grotevant (1997) as having three major components. The first is a set of characteristics by which the individual defines self and is recognized by others within a particular social and historical context. The second component is a sense of coherence as to how the various defining characteristics of the person or personality fit together. The final component of identity refers to a sense of continuity of self in time, place, and relationships. Grotevant et al. (2000, p.382) refer to this as "self-in-context." This is the narrative component of identity. Even as the individual changes over time, there is a sense of continuous personhood. Looking back, a path is recounted in narrative time that describes the journey from one milestone to another. Causal factors that move the person through time may not always be apparent. Regardless, the self is experienced as travelling from past to present and on to an anticipated future.

At the heart of adoptive identity development is the cognitive and affective exploration of possible future selves within the domain of adoption. Adopted adolescents will ask questions such as "Whose child am I?", "What part of me is my genetic endowment and what part is a result of growing up in this adoptive family?", "Why was I really 'given up' for adoption and what does this say about me?", and "Where do I fit in my adoptive and birth families?." All of these questions are asked in the service of answering the core identity question: "Who is the real me?". Adolescents rarely hold to a conclusive response to this question. Instead, they continue to engage in an iterative process of self-exploration in an attempt to integrate the intra psychic sense of self with the demands of family context and other relationships (Graafsma, Bosma, Grotevant & deLevita, 1994).

Grotevant (1997) has offered a developmental sequence for the development of identity. The first stage is marked by a lack of integration of adoption-related material. At this pre-crisis stage, adoption is separated from a sense of self as a fact that is experienced as having little bearing on a sense of self. Grotevant suggests that this is best understood as an act of denial and offers a vignette from Lifton (1994, p.51) to support this conclusion: "Mark . . . at the age of four asked if he could meet the mother he had been told about when he was two and a half. 'It was the first time I wanted and needed something they [his adoptive parents] wouldn't consider. They said that I had to wait until I was eighteen, which is like ninety to a young child. I didn't ask any more questions after that. The fact of my adoption burst like a bubble in my mind, then sealed over. It became important for my sense of coherence as a self to imagine myself as not adopted." While on the surface, this would seem to be an act of denial, an alternative hypothesis is that this vignette represents an example of a young child who lacked full cognitive understanding of what adoption meant. As such, he was not repressing the fact of adoption, but was responding to it in a fashion consistent with his cognitive level of development.

Grotevant's second developmental stage involves a disequilibrating crisis. This may be expressed as either intense reflection and concern about the sense of being adopted or it may be reflected in acting out and other behaviors that on the surface do not seem to be related to adoption. Consistent with Brodzinsky's et al.'s (1984) model of cognitive development and the understanding of the meaning of adoption, pre and young teens have reached a point where they have come to comprehend a fuller view of what it means to be adopted.

The third stage is that of an "integrated sense of identity constructed into a narrative that includes one's adoption circumstances as well as all other aspects of identity important to adult functioning" (Grotevant, 1997, p 18). It is hard to imagine, however, how this is accomplished in a system of adoption that is marked by secrecy and closed records. Few adoptees are able to access enough information to put together a complete adoption narrative. Legislation in most jurisdictions restricts the ability of adoptees to view their adoption records. Furthermore, adoptive parents are under no legal obligation to share adoption-related material with them. All of this serves to heighten the frustration of adoptees who struggle with the integration of adoption into a narrative of self.

This is one of the great paradoxes of adoption. By restricting adoptees' means of integrating adoption into a sense of self, those who support secrecy have heightened the salience and emotional intensity of adoptive identity. Integration requires that one be able to make sense of the past. Having a deficient narrative, marked by gaps in information and limited access to the important players in one's life, leaves many adoptees emotionally frozen and unable to make connections between past and future (Lifton, 1994). If integration is to be the end result of the identity process, then clearly, openness must be an important feature of the adoption landscape.

In sum, all adolescents face the challenge of integrating various cultural categories into their identities. For the most part, when these assigned categories of ethnicity, gender, race, and sexual preference are not outside of the norms for a given community, then there is little difficulty in accepting these assigned definitions of self. However, when an assigned definition such as adoption is part of the identity process, then Grotevant (1997, p.9) has argued, the adoptee must " . . . come to terms" with this given in one's life. "Coming to terms" has the ring of being resigned to membership in a particular identity category. However, the process is, in fact, a much more active one than the phrase would at first imply. While the research and clinical literatures have yet to sort out specific paths to adoptive identity, trends in first hand accounts and clinical reports shed light on this process.

At the centre of the development of adoptive identity is the tension between the basic personality style and temperament of the individual, the evolving sense of self, and the pressures of the social and cultural context that shape identity status. It is here, at the intersection of these forces, that society's and the family's perspectives on adoption interact with adoptees' characteristic ways of responding. Some adoptees will encounter numerous and intense moments of stigmatization of adoptive status while others will not[13]. If their characteristic way of responding is to minimize negative feedback, then in all likelihood, the effects of different-ness, exemplified by adoptive status, will be small. On the other hand, if their characteristic response to stressors is to become more sensitized to such occurrences, then negative feedback concerning adoptive status should result in increased concern with the role that adoption plays in their development of a sense of self. This, however, does not imply that identity formation for adoptees is strictly an intra psychic process. The answer to the question "who am I?" is also strongly shaped by those in the adoptee's world who are affected by the fact that the adoptee is a product of a complex genetic, psychological and social history.

Factors Influencing the Adoptee's Identity Narrative

Similarity or Acceptance of Difference.

One of the fundamental assumptions underlying the place-ment of children into families is that there should be as much similarity as possible between the adoptee and the adoptive par-ents. Much time and effort are given to the selection of adoptive applicants in an attempt to ensure that they will share appearance, aptitudes, abilities and personality styles with the child (Daly &

---

13 See Chapter 3.

Sobol, 1993). For young adoptees, such matching probably plays little part in their sense of connection to adoptive parents for they lack the cognitive skills to be aware of major differences between themselves and their parents. However, by the age of seven, most children have " . . . demonstrated that they understand birth as a process selectively mediating the acquisition of physical traits and learning and nurturance as mediating the acquisition of beliefs" (Solomon, Johnson, Zaitchik & Carey, 1996, p.151). With this newly developed cognitive skill for differentiating genetic from environmental influences, children become more prone to define family in genetic terms (Newman, Roberts & Syre, 1993). Thus, they fall into step with the wider Western cultural definition of family as closely related genetic kin. From the adopted child's perspective, the definition of family defined by nurturance and commitment is now personally challenged by this understanding of family as being genetically based. The child is faced with deciding who are his "real" parents: the adoptive ones or the genetic ones.

For younger children, the answer to this question requires a concrete answer. It must be one set of parents or the other. The child simply lacks the cognitive capacity to recognize the possibility that the answer is both adoptive and genetic parents. If the child chooses the adoptive parents, there must be an active rejection of history and the internalization of the cultural definition of family. On the other hand, if the child accepts a genetic definition of family, then she also has, to all intents and purposes, accepted upon herself the cultural stigma that accompanies this definition. The result is that she must face the belief that she is not a legitimate member of the adoptive family. This can be a frightening position to hold as the child senses that she is living outside of the boundaries of security, connectedness and commitment. It is little wonder that for some adoptees, this period of cognitive maturity also marks the beginning of emotional turmoil around one's place in the family.

It is important not to over generalize. Not all adoptees at this point in development begin to see themselves as being outside of the family. One of the factors that influences which way the child will lean is the degree to which the child shares similarities of appearance, interests, personality and temperament with the adoptive family. If the child does not stand out as markedly different from the adoptive parents, and displays a similar psychological profile, it is easier to think of oneself as being "their kin" (Grand, 2006).

Some adoptees have reported that it is not similarity, per se, that links them to the adoptive family. Rather, it is the willingness of adoptive parents to show an interest in the unique attributes of the adoptee (Grand, 2006). As one adoptee in this study stated:

> "My dad was really uncoordinated. He could hardly throw a ball. He was hopeless at hitting, yet there he was every Saturday in the stands watching me play third base. He really hated sports but he never missed a game. He knew I wanted to hear him cheering for me. He made himself into a sports fan to please me and I loved him for it."

To be sure, there are other factors that will also account for the degree to which adoptees feel connected to their adoptive kin. However, similarity is a robust factor over time. As was documented in Grand's study (2006), adult adoptees reported that the more they felt that they shared similar traits with their adoptive parents, the more positively they rated the success of their adoption. Clearly, similarity places one within the family. Dissimilarity makes the task more challenging. In either case, reactions to the issues of similarity shape the adoptee's sense of being part of a family constructed through adoption. This, in turn, becomes an enduring part of the adoption narrative.

Quality of the Marital Relationship

When we think about adoptees' experiences in their adoptive families, typically attention turns to relationships between the adoptee and each of the parents. However, to fully appreciate the experience of adoptees within their families and their respective emerging personal narratives, it is important to look to other relationships that are part of the adoption constellation. Of all the relationships that touch the life of the adoptee, perhaps the most important one outside of the parent-child relationship is the one between the parents themselves.

Clearly, this relationship has been missing from the adoption literature. Typically, an assumption is made that within adoptive families, adoptees are the only ones who struggle with psychological concerns. Hence, this being an individual matter, there is no need to look beyond their intrapsychic experience. However, emotional processing of information is never undertaken without consideration of the social context in which the information is gathered and made sense of. For adoptees, the most proximal and salient context is the relationship between the marital partners themselves.

Marital satisfaction (Bradbury, Fincham & Beach, 2000) and patterns of partner interaction (Gottman & Notarius, 2000) have been the focus of several decades of research. What has emerged is a relatively clear picture of relationship styles that require adjustment to newly emerging developmental challenges. Not surprisingly, transition to parenthood is of great importance for it sets the stage for later family development. For most couples, becoming parents is both stressful and pleasurable. Counterbalancing the joy of the arrival of a new child, up to 70% of couples report a drop in marital satisfaction. There is an increased risk of depression as parents fall into stereotypic gender roles, and they feel overburdened by the amount of time and effort required to meet household chores and child care needs. Fathers often focus on work. Conversation and sexual relations between the partners decrease, and intimacy becomes a distant memory.

If this marks the challenges of non-adoptive parents, how much more so for those whose families are formed through adoption (Daly, 1988). For adoptive families, there is rarely a delineated period of time that precedes the arrival of the child. We have few rituals to welcome adopted children or to congratulate adoptive parents on their change of status. On one day they are childless, on another they are parents. Predictability at this point of transition is low, to say the least. There is no nine month gestation period. There is no expectation of welcoming a child who might look like themselves or might reflect a family trait. Perhaps most difficult of all, the timing of the appearance is completely out of their hands as control for this transition period is determined by the birth parents, social workers, and attorneys. Is it no wonder then, that many adoptive parents begin the road to parenthood in a state of stress (Daly, 1988; Kirk, 1985).

If the adoptive parents find the means to incorporate the new child into their lives and to rebalance the distribution of roles, responsibilities, and decision making, then marital satisfaction will begin to approach pre placement levels. However, if this transition is not easily mastered, then the interactional dance between the marital partners will become increasingly strained. Communication will tilt toward more negative exchanges. There will be an escalation of high intensity negative affect and increased likelihood that criticism, defensiveness, contempt and stonewalling, what Gottman, Coan, Carrere, and Swanson (1998) have called the four horsemen of the marital apocalypse, will characterize marital interaction.

In such an ascorbic setting, childhood trajectories take a turn toward the development of emotional and behavioral difficulties. Links have been established between marital conflict and childhood distress and depression, withdrawal, social incompetence, poor health outcomes, weak academic attainment and misconduct (Cowan & Cowan, 1987; Easterbrooks, 1987; Rutter, 1971). Cummings, Zahn-Waxler and Radke-Yarrow (1984) found that when children were exposed to angry exchanges between adults, they tended to use more physical aggression as a means of coping. Katz and Gottman (1993) found that hostile interactions between parents led to externalizing child responses, while a hostile and then withdrawing father led to the development of internalizing behaviors in the child. However, if such negative interactions between parents came to a harmonious conclusion, even without resolution of the original reason for the conflict, then the children were left with a sense of emotional security. This was found to occur, regardless of the fact that they had been distressed when observing the initial hostile exchange. All of these reactions to parental conflict have been demonstrated to be mediated by the child's vagal tone, the inherited ability of the parasympathetic nervous system to calm the child (Katz & Gottman, 1995). Children with less reactive nervous systems will be less touched by parental conflict, while those who have more reactive nervous systems will show more pronounced negative sequelae. Finally, it is most important to note that couples who fail to resolve their conflicts tend to let the hostility spill over into their parent-child interactions (Margolin, Christensen & John, 1996), thus, exacerbating the distress of the child.

How does this relate to an adoptee's construction of a personal narrative? For the most part, it depends on the child's understanding of, and attributions for, marital conflict. At the very least, conflicted relations between the marital partners cast a negative tone over the household. Children tend to respond to such a situation by either withdrawing to a safe distance out of the line of fire, or casting themselves into the emotional fray in an attempt to deflect the parents away from engaging each other. In such circumstances, adoptive children, in their efforts to make sense of the conflict, may formulate any one of several different narratives about themselves and their place in the family.

If the child escapes from the conflict, a narrative theme develops around the family being an unsafe place that one should leave as soon as possible. Hence, the child is left with an identity statement that this home, and these people, are not safe to be around. As such, it would not be a good idea to let oneself come to close to them. Such a child would remain vigilant about the risk of proximity to volatile adults. In common psychological parlance we referred to such a child as having an attachment disorder. Clearly, however, the child is not acting abnormally, as attachment theory would suggest. Rather, he is responding adaptively to an unsafe setting. From a narrative perspective, the child tells a personal narrative of isolation and withdrawal in the service of self-protection. It is not a happy narrative but one that attempts to engender a sense of security in what is seen as an unsafe milieu.

A second theme, and one that has even more negative consequences, occurs when the child draws the conclusion that he is the cause of the conflict and without his presence in the family, there would be more harmony. Parents in conflict may directly inform the child that this is the case, or the child may simply make such an assumption. Sadly, this does nothing to assist the child to feel like he has a rightful and positive place in the life of the family, nor does it allow the child to draw the conclusion that he matters to these people (Marshall, 2001). When children, particularly those from abusive backgrounds, believe they are the cause of marital conflict, their narrative is characterized by lowered self worth and a sense of not being valued by important relational figures. The child feels hopeless to be able to change the situation as it is the child as person, not something one has done or said, that the child feels is the cause of the rejection. This places a major stain on identity and creates a personal narrative that will remain difficult to shed over a lifetime.

It is also important to note that adoptees, just like their non adopted cohort, caught within the web of marital conflict, develop trajectories of disorder, the form of which depends on the nature of the conflict, the interpretation of the cause of the conflict, and the child's genetic propensity to respond with either internalizing or externalizing behaviors. If the child has a timid temperament, withdrawal and anxiety will likely be prominent. If the child has inherited lowered impulse control, then acting out would be the expected result. In narrative terms, the parents will have difficulty seeing the child as responding normally to an abnormal situation and instead may ground their understanding of the child in terms of psychopathology and weak genetic stock. If the child incorporates such an understanding into his narrative, the first chapters of a story of psychopathology will be written.

In the end, the marital relationship provides the setting in which narratives of worth, trust and predictability are constructed. If the relationship between parents is strong, caring and without violence, the child has an opportunity to model positive parental styles of interaction and to take on a sense of self that is affirming. If conflict is high, not only will the child learn negative styles of interaction but will also come to see that such styles are normative. These experiences will be incorporated into his sense of self and will be reflected in a negative narrative of worth.

Finally, it is important to keep in mind that the effects of marital conflict are not unidirectional. Bringing any child into a family constellation will result in some degree of stress as the parents learn to cope with incorporating the new member into the family. For adoptive families, the new child is truly a stranger. Older adopted children, particularly those who have been abused or have experienced multiple placements prior to coming into the adoptive home, could be expected to be challenging. They might not trust that this placement will be a permanent home no matter what the adoptive parents do or say. They may be unable, at first, to allow their guards to drop physically or emotionally. It is, therefore, not surprising that adoptive parents, who have not had previous parenting experience or are older and set in their ways, will find their new children to be quite a challenge. In such a setting, the frustrations of the parents can easily irrupt into marital conflict as the parents struggle to cope with their new child.

Thus, marital conflict is either a cause of childhood distress or is a consequence of the child's distress. In either scenario, we see the systemic dance that takes place between children and parents.

Overall, the research indicates that most adoptive families find spontaneous means for working their way through the difficult steps of placement and family adaptation. However, for those who do not, it is clear that for the child to be able to rewrite a personal narrative that includes trust, intimacy and affection, there must be a change in one or several constituent parts of the constellation. Typically, when the children are not faring well, they are sent for therapy. However, a systemic understanding of adoption would suggest that marital therapy with the aim of bringing about the rebalancing of all relationships in the family would be of equal importance for the child. This is where most professional thinking in adoption breaks down. We ground our theoretical understanding and intervention practices to directly changing the child when in fact, often times, it is the marital relationship that is in need of modification. It is only by taking a systemic view of the family, and recognizing that all members of the adoption constellation are impacted by the emotional gravitational pull of all its constituent parts, that we will be able to meet the developmental needs of an adopted child. Therefore, when we think about post adoption services for adoptive families, we should not consider "fixing the child." We should work toward rebalancing the interrelationship between the elements of the constellation. To this end, marriage and family therapy must be part of the package of post adoption services.

Social Network Acceptance

For adoptees, the message concerning where one legitimately belongs, not only comes from the nuclear, adoptive family. It also is drawn from the wider social networks that adoptees occupy.

One of the most important of these networks is the school system. Most adopted adolescents are able to describe how the topic of adoption was dealt with within the context of the school. Typically, a teacher would ask the class to produce a family tree. Knowing that they were members of two families, the birth and the adopted one, often put them at odds with the requirements of this classroom task. It highlights the fact that their route to family formation was clearly not the norm. In a similar fashion, teachers' explanations of conception, gestation and birth usually end with "mommy and daddy taking the baby home." However, in infant adoption placements, the birth mother does not physically accompany the infant on this journey. Instead, someone else "chooses" the infant and becomes the parent. The reality for adoptees is that their narrative may be stigmatized and perceived as deviant.

Many adolescent adoptees also have emotionally tinged memories of how the facts of their adoption were received by friends and peers. If others expressed little interest or concern about the adoption, this would typically result in the adoptee attributing less significance to the status of adoption. However, when adoption was seen by peers as a character fault or at the least, a sign of an ignoble beginning, then the adoptee was faced with the challenge of incorporating a stigmatized characteristic into one's identity.

In a parallel fashion, the recollection of the acceptance of the adoptee into the wider adoptive family has important consequences for the development of adoptive identity. Perhaps the most salient marker of acceptance is whether extended, adoptive family members choose to use the term "adopted" as an adjective in describing the adoptee's familial relationships. Being referred to as the adopted child of the parents or the adopted cousin, grandchild or niece signifies that the adoptee is not a full member of the family but is one who sits on the outer ring of the family constellation. Likewise, receiving gifts of a different value than consanguineous kin or not being recognized in the will of senior members of the family as a rightful recipient of family heirlooms clearly sets the adoptee apart from other family members. On the other hand, if language and behavior do not mark the adoptee off as an illegitimate member of the family, there is evidence to suggest that the adoptee will invest less in a definition of self as an outsider who does not have a rightful place within the adoptive family (Grand, 2001). This is not to say that in such circumstance, adoption will not have a part in the structure of identity of adoptees. Acceptance by the wider adoptive family network serves as a moderating variable, affecting the degree of salience that is attributed to the definitional aspects of self found in one's adoptive status.

The preplacement history of adoptees who came into their family as older children, can be highly significant. In the case of severe physical, sexual or emotional abuse, there may be difficulty in remembering these events as they remain outside of conscious awareness. Multiple placements and caretakers also may be difficult to recall as places and circumstances often blend together. For very young children, lacking the ability to verbally code the memories of these early events, all that remains in adolescence is a murky view of chronology. However, single experiences or objects may be recalled such as a favorite teddy bear, a trip to the park or a particular caretaker. These stand out against the less articulated and painful moments of the past. Not being able to recall these earlier and difficult events, some adoptees are left with vague feelings of discomfort and diminished self worth. They are aware that something has contributed to these feelings but are unable to say exactly what it might be. The end result for the construction of narrative is that their story is colored by their perceived reception within the social networks surrounding their nuclear adoptive family.

Openness and the Emotional Valence of Communication

As adolescents go about constructing a core adoptive identity, they gather into an integrative narrative the multitude of facts that they have accumulated across development. Some of these facts are historical in nature, detailing such events as their place of birth, the age of their birth parents at placement, the circumstances under which the adoption took place, and the adoptive parents' motivation for adopting. They may remember the moment when they initially became aware of being adopted. Recollections of the first and subsequent renditions of the adoption story offered by their adoptive parents are also common experiences.

While these facts comprise the building blocks of an adoptive identity, it is the degree of openness and emotional quality of parental communication that serve as the mortar for the adoption narrative.

In his seminal work, Shared Fate, (1965), David Kirk offered an insightful consideration of adoptive family process. He suggested that for an adoptive family to successfully engage the experience of adoption, it was necessary for two things to occur. The first was that the family, and primarily the adoptive parents had to acknowledge the differences between adoptive families and those who followed a consanguineous route to family formation. Acknowledgement of difference meant that there must be a recognition that the tasks of adoptive family life are not the same as those found in consanguineous families. On the practical side, this required adoptive parents to deal with their own sense of loss and grief around infertility. Adoptees who felt a sense of loss of origins were also given permission to engage in the range of emotions that accompanied this loss. It meant recognizing that adoptive children were not necessarily going to be reflections of their adoptive parents in terms of attitudes, aptitudes, temperament, appearance or abilities. Acknowledgement of difference also carried with it the perception that their children might follow a different route than non-adopted adolescents as they came to terms with the demands of individuation and separation, and established a sense of identity that incorporated a multilayered history of origins and subsequent development.

Families who denied difference between themselves and consanguineous families essentially truncated the range of topics allowed within family conversations. To deny difference was to say that the adoptee was truly "as if born" to the adopting parents. It was to suppress conversation about history and origins that took the adoptee outside of the adoptive family. Feelings about loss of origins for adoptees and fertility for adoptive parents were not to be expressed. In extreme denial of difference, adoptees were punished for displaying interest in or initiating any activity that would lead them toward renewing contact with their birth family.

While acknowledgement and denial of difference mark the extremes of family communication, most adoptive families operate between these extremes, choosing to lean in one direction or the other, depending on the current developmental tasks of the family.

During the early days of the adoption, denial of difference was very much the norm, as adoptive parents responded to the excitement and joy of incorporating a new member into their nuclear family. The last things that most adoptive parents were thinking of at this time were the needs of the birth parents or the fact that their new child had a genetic history that may prove to be of some importance at a later point in development. The essential matter in these early moments of the adoption is that they have *their* child. Most naturally, they do not want to be reminded that they share this child, in some fashion with another family. However, by the time of the first telling of the adoption story, adoptive parents must acknowledge the difference between themselves and consanguineous families. It is difficult at this point to deny the reality that the child does not share their genetic heritage. How parents chose to convey this fact, and even of more importance, the tone of this and subsequent tellings will do much to affect the child's sense of embeddedness within the family.

I have met families in which the adoption story was told once and then never revisited again. The parents believed that they had fulfilled their responsibilities: they had conveyed to the child the fact that an adoption had occurred. They felt no need to dwell on this episode and conveyed the message to their children in subtle and not so subtle ways that the subject was closed to any future discussion. Any breach of this decision was to be understood by the parents as an act of disloyalty and rejection of the commitment they had made to the child.

Other families permitted continued conversation about the adoption and the birth family, but did so in a highly charged and hostile manner. They recognized the need to speak of the adoption but were unable to deal with their own strong unresolved feelings around fertility and entitlement to parent. Thus, whenever the adoptee initiated a conversation about the adoption, he was met with a strong, negative emotional response from one or both parents.

It should also be pointed out that there are times in the course of an adoption when adoptees do not wish to talk about or recognize that they have come from parents other than the adoptive ones. Lifton (1994) has described this reluctance to engage the topic of the adoption as an act of denial. While this sometimes may be the case, I would suggest that the primary motivation for such reluctance has more to do with the fact that the adoptee is simply engaged in other, more demanding, developmental tasks. Adoptive status is not the only thing in the life of those who have been adopted that defines them as individuals. Depending on the unique proclivities of adoptees, and their level of development, social relationships, recreational and academic pursuits, and the identity-defining aspects of gender and ethnicity will, at times, capture their attention to an equal or greater degree than the issue of adoption. Being adopted does not necessarily mean that one must always be preoccupied with adoption. It is primarily when the familial context overstresses the importance of adoption or in contrast, fails to respond in a sensitive manner that the adoptee's feelings around connectedness to the adoptive family will be most salient.

An example would be helpful here. Almost all parents, regardless of whether they are adoptive parents or not, struggle with the emerging sexuality of their children. At the point where adolescents become sexually active, parents are faced with the challenge of encouraging either abstinence or sexually responsible behavior. For adoptive parents, their adolescents' sexual behavior provides an additional challenge. Many adoptive parents came to adoption because of their own infertility. Their adolescent children are usually unaware of their own fertility status, but the assumption is that they are fertile until proven otherwise. Hence, the adolescent represents to the parent a state of being that has been missing in the life of the parent. Furthermore, sexually active adopted teens remind adoptive parents of the circumstances that may have made the child available for adoption in the first place. For many adoptive parents, there is great fear that their children will repeat the pattern of behavior of their birth parents and find themselves with an unplanned pregnancy. These issues around fertility and pregnancy are highly charged and usually engender strong emotional responses.

Adoptive parents, in these circumstances are caught in an attributional bind. They do not know how to attribute or explain the behavior of their children. Is being sexually active a result of normal adolescent development, their parenting style, the genetic expression of birth parent proclivities ("bad seed"), or the act of an adoptee trying to understand the earlier experience of birth parents?

Too often, in the course of heated discussions about sexual behavior, adoptees have told me that their adoptive parents have compared their behavior to that of their birth mothers. This is said in an attempt to caution the adolescent. However, the result of such statements is that the adoptee is given two negative messages: If the birth mother had acted differently, then the adoptee would never have been born; and if the birth mother was morally lacking, then the adoptee, being her genetic kin, is also lacking. So, what started out as a conversation about responsible sexual behavior degenerates into a confrontation around family history and the worth of the adoptee and her genetic kin. This may not have been the intent of the adoptive parents but sadly, it is not an uncommon outcome.

And here arises another paradox. If the birth family is disparaged, the adoptee, sharing DNA with them, also feels under attack. This heightened identification with one's origins results in the adoptee feeling a more positive connection to the birth family. This is matched by a shift away from a sense of alliance with the adoptive parents (Grand, 2006). Given that the adolescent pregnancy literature has identified closeness to custodial parents as the most important factor in decreasing the risk of adolescent pregnancy (Miller, Benson, & Galbraith, 2001), adoptive parents may have inadvertently assisted in creating the very situation that they were trying to avoid. They may also have lessened the adoptee's identification with the adoptive family.

Adoptive Parents as Gatekeepers of the Adoption Story

Until an adoptee has received identifying information and the adoption files, or has had a reunion, the adoptive parents are the primary custodians of the adoption story. After all, they were there at the beginning of the adoption. They might have met the birth parents or been given background information pertaining to the birth family. Being the gatekeepers of the adoption story, the adoptive parents are in a powerful position indeed. How they utilize this power will have a telling effect upon the adoptee's sense of connection to them and hence, will have an impact upon the development of adoptive identity of their children.

Some adoptive parents see the adoption story as a precious gift that they wish to share with their children. Beginning with the first telling and with all subsequent renditions, they provide the facts of the story in a manner that is commensurate with the cognitive and emotional level of the adoptee. The story is told calmly and with respect for all parties. There is no attempt to embarrass the adoptee or engender feelings of gratitude either for having adopted the child or for sharing the story. These parents see the story as part of the birth right of the adoptee. They are sensitive to the emotional reactions of their child and are willing to accept the pain and sense of loss that many adoptees experience when confronting the realities that have brought them into the adoptive family. Successful sharing of the adoption story also means that adoptive parents are open and willing to talk about all aspects of the adoption, even those parts that touch their own sense of loss and grief. This does not mean that it is necessary to always have the telling at the top of the family's agenda but it does require that the adoptee not feel fearful about the topic of adoption. In fact, it is accessibility to the story, and to a slightly lesser extent, the emotional valence of the telling, that have an influence upon adoptees' subsequent development of a personal narrative adoptive identity. Parents must be willing to acknowledge that their adopted children will follow a different route to identity formation in that they must go beyond the boundaries of the adoptive family to ground themselves in a life story. Adopted parents must also be open to adoption-related conversation and not see it as a betrayal of their commitment to their children. In doing so, they will have a positive influence upon both their child's sense of well being and perception of the success of the adoption (Grand, 2006).

However, if the adoption is a difficult topic to bring up or if conversation is sanctioned but results in anger or hostility, then the adoptee will see his adoptive status as a negative quality, and will feel distance between himself and his adoptive family. In such circumstances, in answer to the identity question, "who am I?", it is not easy to say "I am the child of the people who have brought me into their home and raised me." They may be seen as caretakers, guardians or those who have altered one's life course but it will be difficult to see them as nurturing parents. They will be perceived as taking liberties with the most crucial component of identity for most adoptees: the story of who I am; how I have travelled to this family; and what connection I am entitled to have with my family of origin.

This is a difficult notion for some adoptive parents to grasp. Fearing that too much discussion will orient the adoptee in the direction of the birth family, they choose to limit conversation about origins and subsequently create the very situation that they had hoped to avoid: the adoptee's failure to identify with them and an increase in the salience and connection to the birth family. Adoptive parents who are open and accessible, on the other hand, typically recognize that it is not an "us versus them" situation. Sensitive parents recognize that successful development of an identity requires that the adoptee be able to integrate both adoptive and birth families into one's narrative. In order to accomplish this, adoptees require the adoptive parents to co-construct their story with them. They also need access to enough information to build the story in the first place. If the adoptive parents do not possess relevant information, if they are unwilling to share the knowledge that they have, or if the adoptee does not have access to the birth family and his adoption records, then he will have to face the dilemma of how to build an identity within a deficient narrative (Lifton, 1994). Cohler (1982) has suggested that the inability to construct an integrated narrative, that gives meaning to one's history, may result in the experiencing of psychological distress. The state of the research literature does not allow for strong statements on this matter (Grotevant, 1997). However, clinical and case study material would suggest a deficient narrative is clearly a risk factor for adoptees who struggle to construct a coherent account of their life stories.

Access to Open Adoption Records

To fully understand the place that legislation plays in the shaping of personal adoptive narratives, we must begin by examining how legislation is grounded within cultural discourse about reunion and access to information. Fortunately, three recent surveys, two American (Dave Thomas Foundation for Adoption, 2002; and Evan B. Donaldson Adoption Institute, 1997) and one Canadian (Miall & March, 2005) shed some light on this issue.

In the United States, there is widespread support for the notion of reunion. In the Evan B. Donaldson Adoption Institute Survey (1997), 68% of respondents thought that reunion was beneficial for adult adoptees. The same figure was found in the Dave Thomas Foundation for Adoption Survey (2002). Interestingly, there is much less support for the idea that reunion is a good experience for birth parents, with 56% and 49% taking a positive view of reunion for birth parents. In the Canadian survey, Miall and March (2005) found that an overwhelming number of Canadians (91%) thought that reunions resulted in positive outcomes for adoptees and birth family. Unfortunately, they did not differentiate between an evaluation of the experience for adoptees and birth parents in separate questions. Nevertheless, we can conclude that in North America the idea of reunion is favorably held.

One would think, therefore, that steps leading to a reunion would also be evaluated in a parallel manner. However, the picture that emerges is not straightforward. Of the Canadians sampled, 77% supported the idea of unrestricted access by adoptees to personal identifying information, including the name of the birth parents. A reciprocal access to identifying information for birth parents, though, was not supported. Only 45% of respondents stated that birth parent access to information be granted, but only if the adoptee gave permission for its release. Unfortunately, these questions were not part of the American surveys and so we can only surmise similar possible findings. Thus, what we have is a confused picture. On the one hand, there is strong support for the positive value of reunion. On the other, at least in Canada, and probably in the United States, there is support only for adoptees to receive unrestricted identifying information. Birth parents, however, are seen to have the right to obtain such information, only if adoptees give permission for its release.

How does this play out in legislation? For the most part, there is a split in the legislative responses to the opening of adoption records. In Canada, a majority of the provinces have now granted adoptees and birth parents access to identifying information with the proviso that if either party files an information veto, the file will not be opened to the other party. In the United States, in those few jurisdictions where there is access to information, this has only been granted to adult adoptees and not birth parents who continue to have no right to information about the children, now adults, whom they brought into the world.

The negative effective of such restrictive legislation on personal adoptive narratives is obvious: Those adoptees who have been blocked from access to information are potentially left with a deficient narrative. They may have sparse information about the first chapter of their lives as the result of adoptive parents' acts of omission, the leaving out of details they do not wish to share. Adoptees may also have false information as a result of acts of commission, performed by either adoptive parents or social workers who intentionally provided a non-veridical history . In either case, the opening chapter of such narratives remains incomplete to say the least. Adoptees in such circumstances typically feel helpless to rectify the situation as they have no legislative right to their own story and the details of how they came into the world through one family and grew up with another. The emotional, consequence of this is either depression as a result of having no where to turn, or anger and frustration for the fact that while the information exists in a file, they have no right to know who they were when they were born.

Typically, when politicians defend their position of keeping files closed, they speak in the name of birth parents, and particularly birth mothers. They argue that birth mothers were promised anonymity. These women, it is said, remain in fear, so many years after placement, that their deeds will be exposed not only to the adoptee but to those in their current family circle. If the legislative hearings in Ontario are representative of the experiences of birth mothers, then a very different picture emerges. For some birth mothers, there was a promise of anonymity but a perusal of documents severing the legal ties between parent and child will show that no mention whatsoever appears concerning future access to information. In fact, some birth mothers reported that they were told that if they consented to the placement they would have the future right to know the changed name of their child as an adult. Again, nothing to this effect appears in the documentation. One is led to wonder why legislators, particularly males, feel such a strong need to protect these women from being known by their offspring. After all, we do not hear an outcry from birth mothers demanding that their anonymity be preserved. Could it be that the legislators themselves have something to hide? To loosely paraphrase Shakespeare, "me thinks they doth protect too much." Do they think that secrecy will enhance adoptive family life? That adoptees will forget about their origins? That secrecy will insure the legitimacy of the role of adoptive parent and preserve the security of facilitators of adoption?

If they believe this, they are blatantly ignoring the research evidence that points in the opposite direction. Openness frees relationships to a wider range of possibilities to meet personal needs (Grotevant & McRoy, 2003). Adoptive parental support for search and reunion brings adoptees and adoptive parents closer together (Sobol & Cardiff, 1983). Significantly, not searching or not being able to search is not a sign of adoptee disinterest. Rather, such decisions are typically linked to concern about others' feelings to the detriment of one's own (Sobol & Cardiff, 1983). What is equally troubling is that those who oppose open records never address the negative consequence of their obstructive behavior for those seeking access to personal and defining information. They have a blind spot to this issue, remaining instead, focused on the cowering birth mother, a phenomenon that is more myth than reality.

To conclude, I believe that no one is entitled to a relationship, but everyone is entitled to a veridical history. Adoptees must have the same rights to identifying information as their non-adopted peers: a truthful birth registration, not one that has been changed to preserve the notion that adoptive parents are the consanguineous progenitors of the adoptee. To fear the truth results in the need to distort relationships in the service of preserving a lie. If adoptees are to make peace with the journey that others have placed them on, then they must be able to write the beginnings of their narrative. In a similar fashion, birth parents, many of whom have narratives that are frozen at the end of chapter one, need to know what happened to their children. To block such information is cruel and inexcusable.

Narrative Integration

Narrative Structure

As the above discussion has detailed, narrative adoptive identity is shaped by both the totality of life experiences before and after placement, and the personal interpretation of the meaning of these events. As such, no two adoptive narratives will ever be exactly the same. Furthermore, given the developmental nature of these personal renditions of self in history, it should be clear that they are expected to change over time as content and contexts evolve.

Grotevant et al., (2000) have argued that adoptive identity can be conceptualized along three structural dimensions. The first of these is internal consistency. "A narrative is highly consistent when it includes examples that support personal theories or themes, and synthesizing statements that pull the narrative together." It is inconsistent "…when it has few or no examples, lacks synthesizing statements, or includes contradictions that are unexplained or unrecognized." The second structural dimension is flexibility: the degree to which issues are possibly seen by others. Those with flexible narratives embrace the complexity of the relationships and historical themes. On the other hand, when one has an inflexible narrative, the story line is rigid and narrowly focused on one's own perspective on relationships and history. The final structural component of an adoptive narrative identity concerns the degree or depth to which adoptees will explore what adoption actually means, how actively they seek further information and how they engage in decision-making. This component is reflected in whether the person contrasts old and new ways of thinking about her adoption, contrasts her perspective with other constellation members' perspectives, teases out what it means to be adopted, questions previous views and is willing to struggle for new perspectives and facts.

These structural aspects of narrative adoptive identity are primarily the end result of the interplay of the degree of parental willingness to be open to conversations about adoption, the emotional valence of these discussions, as well as the amount of detailed information they are able to convey. If the parent is open, supportive and authenticating in feedback, and provides information which matches the adoptee's emotional and cognitive stage of development, then one would expect to find consistent, flexible, in-depth narratives. On the other hand, if parents feel they have fulfilled their responsibilities by having told the child that he is adopted, convey information in negative tones, and give nothing but the bare bones of story detail, then narrative identity would, in all likelihood, be blunted.

However, there is more to a narrative identity than simply structure, per se. There is also content. At one level the two cannot easily be separated for without content, narrative structure will always remain somewhat inflexible, inconsistent and lacking in exploration. Content provides for the possibility of opening up the narrative. As an example of this relationship between structure and content, Grotevant et al., (2000) have demonstrated that parents' facilitation of contact between adoptive and birth families assists in the development of stronger and more positive identity narratives for their adopted children.

Narrative Themes

When thinking about narrative content, we must distinguish between the gathering of historical facts and the super ordinate concepts that organize and provide meaning for the facts of one's adoption. Identity, perhaps the major core issue, has been described above. The remainder of this chapter will detail the other super ordinate concepts, focusing on the work of Silverstein and Rozsia (2001). These core issues provide the potential themes of one's narrative and the outline of one's sense of self as an adoptee and a person in the world. The extent to which these themes are present in individual narratives will differentiate one adoptee's experience from another. Not all themes will be emphasized, nor will adoptees construct a narrative that necessarily reflects the negative end points of these dimensions.

Loss. At the center of adoptive narrative identity is the notion of loss. Birth parents have lost a child to another family, adoptive parents have lost the possibility of raising a consanguineous child, and of course, adoptees have multiple losses: the family of their birth, the opportunity to be raised by a "real" parent as defined and constructed by society, the right to an unrestricted set of veridical facts about their origins and early development, the right to be treated under the law in the same manner as those who have not been adopted, and most importantly, the right to access a continuing relationship with those with whom they share DNA.

These are historical facts. The pertinent issue, however, is not that they happened, but how they are experienced. For some adoptees, the loss is somewhat diminished by the replacement family and the support they have received since placement. For others, loss defines their very being as all encounters are seen through this lens. A third group claims little sense of loss, believing that what followed the initial loss more than makes up for the missing pieces of their history. Whether this is simply denial, as Lifton (1994) believes, or is truly reflective of an identity narrative devoid of a theme of loss is difficult to determine. I would suggest that it depends on the degree of empathy expressed by the adoptee for the losses of others in the constellation. If the adoptee has little awareness or compassion for the birth family's sense of loss, or fails to perceive the losses of the adoptive parents, then I would expect that the adoptee would not incorporate an articulated sense of loss into her own personal adoptive narrative. However, if there is an appreciation of others' losses, then a failure to experience a personal sense of loss is less likely reflective of denial, and is simply the result of a process that in weighing losses and gains, the latter are experienced as far more salient than the former.

From a developmental perspective, it is important to remember that loss is not a static characteristic of one's narrative but is a process that ebbs and flows across time. For example, loss is experienced differently during the early days following placement than it is following an adoptee's birthing of her own child. Developmental transition points, thus, serve as moderators of the salience of the loss of the missing other. An inflexible narrative, which is not modified with changing context, leaves the adoptee unable to find new and more adaptive ways to incorporate the undeniable fact of loss into one's narrative.

Rejection. If loss is the fundamental historic fact of adoptive narrative identity, then rejection is the emotional qualifier of this fact. Most older adoptees are able to state unequivocally that they were rejected by their birth parents. On a surface level, the facts speak for themselves. They were born into one family. They grew up in a different family. Someone or some event led to the rejection of their presence in the family of their birth. Most adoptees have difficulty providing a full and complete rendition of this bare bones outline. This is not surprising, particularly if it occurred in an era of secrecy and closed adoption. Thus, in the absence of contradictory information, which would lead to a much more nuanced understanding of the events of birth and subsequent placement of the child, all the adoptee would likely conclude is that the adoption was the result of the rejection of the child by a birth parent. Contrast this situation with full and respectful open adoption where the child has an ongoing relationship with birth kin. There are opportunities to challenge the rejection theme by considering the unique set of circumstances that led to placement. Furthermore, having the birth parent in the life of the adoptee is living proof that rejection was not necessarily the motivation behind placement. Sharon Rozsia, a seasoned and insightful adoption professional, has brought this point alive when she reinterpreted the phrase "the birth mother gave up the child for adoption" to mean not rejection, but rather, she finally "gave up" in the face of all the powerful forces that tried to take her child from her care. Thus, without the birth mother in the life of the adoptee, how could one not conclude that rejection is a major theme in one's narrative identity.

Shame and guilt. The history of adoption in North America has been rife with strategies for the management of guilt and shame. Early legislation, policies and practices were directed at hiding the public shame of the inner circle of the adoption constellation. Adoptive parents wanted altered birth documents and the attaching of their family name to the adoptee as a means of protecting themselves from public scrutiny of their infertile status.

Consanguineous parents were told that their soiled identity status as unmarried progenitors would be cleansed of its moral stain if they simply disappeared out of history. And what of adoptees? For many, adoption was experienced as a fact that must be hidden in an attempt to preserve the myth that the adoptive family was no different than a consanguineous one. But in yielding to this myth, adoptees were left with the feeling that there was clearly something wrong with them, otherwise, why would they have found themselves in such circumstances instead of being raised by their birth kin.

From a narrative perspective, guilt may be written into the script in two main ways: Firstly, as possessing some personal characteristic that made it impossible for the birth family to continue to act in the role of active caretakers; alternatively, failing to meet the needs of adoptive parents who have stated that they have given up so much to create an adoptive family.

Shame, on the other hand, enters the narrative as an emotional theme of diminished identity status. While the early telling of the adoption tale may be filled with the joy of being the "special" and "chosen" child, at a later point, believing that one is "illegitimate" or the result of an immoral or dubious coupling, leaves some adoptees with the sense that at their core, they are not good. Such a negative self evaluation often results in one of two extremes: Either the adoptee acts out this shame-based identity, proving that authenticity can at least be found in deviance; or the adoptee takes on a strategy for removing such an identity by going beyond the limit to always meet the expectations of the adoptive family. Fortunately, most adoptees find a middle ground between these two extremes to manage their shameful feelings about origins and status.

Grief. In my 35 years of work as a clinical psychologist, perhaps the issue that adoptive parents have the most difficulty dealing with is the grief experienced by their adopted children. The typical scenario sounds like this: "My child has come from difficult circumstances. I have taken them from all that and given them a home of love and material security. Why do they have to grieve? Their birth parents abused or abandoned them. It's not grief they should feel, its gratitude." In such a scenario, parents fail to recognize the multiple losses of the adoptee, and their own role in thwarting the adoptee's opportunity to find adaptive means of coping with this profound sense of loss. And what are these losses? The loss of relationships, the loss of a self that could have been if one had been raised in different circumstances and the loss of an historical and genetic sense of self.

Adoptees grieve in many ways. Sometimes, it is expressed directly, for example, as tears shed for the missing parent, foster parent or other loved one. For other adoptees, grief is experienced as a sadness that pervades all aspects of life. The child's behavior is marked by diminished activity, daydreaming, lack of initiative and sighing. There are adoptees whose grief spills over into rage at the felt injustice of their life's trajectory. Some adoptees' strategy of coping with their grief is to try and understand it at an experiential level by putting themselves in circumstances that they imaged their birth parents were in prior to the placement. Finally, there are adoptees who manage their grief by denying its existence. Outwardly, they display nothing that would indicate emotional turmoil, nor do they report moments of profound sadness tied to their reflections upon their histories. However, careful, non threatening questioning of this latter group usually yields examples of the adoptee being surprised by sudden, although typically private, expressions of grieving.

Failure to address the grief openly and in a supportive manner leaves the adoptee with a narrative rendition of self as a person alone in the world, who, if he is to survive, must not count on others but must fall back on one's own resources. This emotionally isolates some adoptees, leaving them unable or unwilling to form close and intimate relationships. The narrative consequence of grieving alone is that the person incorporates the role of the griever into his story line.

To fully understand the experience of grief, it must be recognized that it is not just an intrapersonal phenomenon. It also is an interpersonal one as well. Before, exploring how this is integrated into a narrative theme for adoptees, it is necessary to turn to another community that has struggled with grief.

In the late 1980's, Ken Doka, a sociologist, began studying the experiences of partners of AIDS patients who had succumbed to their illness. He noted a significant and reoccurring pattern: these partners found themselves on the outside of the mourning rituals of the family of the deceased. The family failed to recognize the partner as an important person in the life of the deceased. Furthermore, partners received no public recognition of their grief nor any social support for its amelioration. This led Doka (1989, 2002) to define these experiences as disenfranchised grief: the "grief that results when a person experiences a significant loss and the resultant grief is not openly acknowledged, socially validated, or publicly mourned. In short, although the individual is experiencing a grief reaction, there is no social recognition that the person has a right to grieve or a claim for social sympathy or support (Doka, 2008, p. 223)".

Evelyn Robinson (2000), an Australian social worker recognized the importance of this concept for the understanding of the experiences of mothers[14] who gave birth to children who subsequently

14 I have struggled with finding appropriate and respectful language to designate women and men whose children were adopted by others. Up until placement, or the signing of papers severing the legal ties, I have simply used the terms "mother" and "father." After this juncture, things become more complicated. Some have suggested we use the term "first mother", while in the literature we find reference to "birth mother", "genetic mother," "biological mother," and "natural mother." I have chosen to use the term "birth mother." It recognizes that the legal ties between child and parent have been severed while still maintaining the historical truth that someone other than the adoptive mother gave birth to the child. It also highlights that carrying and giving birth to a child results for most in an enduring emotional relationship with the child, even though mother and child are separated by law and circumstance. I use this term advisably because I recognize that it could be taken as a derogatory term that simple recognizes the mother's incubating role in the birth of the child. I

were adopted. In forceful and articulate strokes, she painted a picture of the profound sense of loss that these women experienced and the denial by all who came in contact with them that they were living with profound and enduring grief.

Robinson recognized that most women whose children were placed for adoption were viewed by the wider society as deviants for becoming pregnant without a supporting partner or family, and for breaking a bond which is viewed in our society as natural, if not primal. Therefore, these birth mothers had no right to publically mourn nor was their grief to be publically supported. The turning away from birth mothers also served the interests of those facilitating the adoption and those who adopted the child. By doing so, they were less encumbered by guilt associated with their contribution to the birth mother's grief and pain. Thus, birth mothers were encouraged to act as if the birth and subsequent placement had never happened and to "get on with life."

As evidence of the denial of the reality of loss, one needs look no further than the laws governing maternity benefits. In most jurisdictions, there are simply no benefits available for birth mothers. At the same time, we find adoptive parent groups lobbying legislators to increase benefits for themselves, arguing that it is stressful for adoptive parents to bring a new child into their lives. Furthermore, to deny them benefits equivalent to other parents would delegitimize their experience as real parents struggling with real problems. But for all the lobbying of this group, not a word is offered for birth mothers who not only have to recovered from the physical demands of pregnancy and birthing but must also immediately re-enter their daily lives without any recognition or amelioration of their profound sense of loss and grief.

I believe that this concept of disenfranchised grief also extends to adoptive parents and adoptees.

---

hope that soon we will have better terms that truly capture the historical and emotional realities of those whose children were placed for adoption.

For adoptive parents, the loss and grief are primarily focused upon the loss of the child who never was. With each developmental milestone achieved by the adoptive family, the parents are reminded of the child they were unable to give birth to and the experiences that they were denied as a result of their infertility. What makes it particularly difficult for these parents is that this loss, and its accompanying grief, cannot be publically articulated for to do so would mean that they would be stating that adoptive and consanguineous families are not equivalent. It would be a public admittance that adoptive families are truly fictive (Schneider, 1980) and that the joys and rewards of such family life fall short of the ideal. And so, adoptive parents carry this grief in their hearts, never to share it with those who might understand or offer the healing touch of empathy and support.

How does this impact the adoptee's narrative? By failing to find means of identifying and articulating the grief they might feel, parents are likely stunted in their ability to respond to the grief of their children for to address the pain of another is to open oneself to one's own personal grief. By not being available to their children, by turning away from the signs of their children's distress and only seeing intentional withdrawal or uncontrollable outbursts, they deny a source of such behavior, the child's own disenfranchised grief. Here we come to the heart of adoptee-parent relationship: the experience of being able to freely and safely share intimate feelings of loss and grief without a sense of guilt for not meeting the other's expectations.

No matter how much an adoptive parent tries to fill the gap left by the separation of a child from her family of origin, the fact remains that the child has lost the family of her birth and the adoptive family can never be a perfect replacement, substituting one family for another. For the child, the question remains why the connection between herself and her birth family has been severed. Was it because she was not a good enough child to be kept within the bounds of the birth family? Was she responsible for the birth parent's loss of parenting rights? And the questions extend beyond history to a current sense of identity. What kind of person would she be if she had not been adopted? Was that potential self lost forever? Would she be happier if she had grown up in her family of origin? Would she feel loved and protected by them? And most importantly, would anyone ever know or want to know how much she might feel the pain of not having answers to these questions? Would she always have to carry this emotional baggage alone, without anyone sharing the load, providing a place of refuge and support without condition or restriction?

How parents respond to these questions is part of the paradox of adoption: to answer them fully is to admit that adoptive family life is different than consanguineous family life. Parents must face up to the fact that these questions of difference must be addressed before they will be able to approach a place where family life is less marked by an overlay of difference. In other words, the family must be different in order not to be different, a confusing paradox indeed.

If parents turn their backs on their children by refusing to respond in a supportive way to all of these existential questions, then the child will draw the conclusion that she is very much alone in the world, even though there might be many people claiming to love and support her. This commanding narrative theme will permeate the stories one tells oneself. "No one truly knows me or what I am feeling. To walk in the world with such pain is so difficult. I send out all of these signals of my distress but others only recognize their surface features – I'm acting out or withdrawing. They never ask me why." For some, this rendition of the narrative is colored by anger, for others, by profound sadness and growing depression.

For one group of adoptees, the management of disenfranchised grief comes in the form of trying to be the perfect child who does all that is asked of her. She becomes a high achiever with a need to always be in control and be able to predict what is about to happen. This takes a great deal of psychological energy but has the effect of focusing the adoptee away from the internal experience that can be so painful. It is management by distraction, the narrative result of which are self statements about needing to rely on oneself, staying in control so that emotions are held in check, and of not getting too close to others for fear they will break through such strongly held defenses.

Disenfranchised grief is not a necessary condition of adoption nor is it an issue that all adoptees must face. It is the consequence when members of the adoption constellation close themselves off to others' experience of loss and pain. If adoptive parents are willing to let themselves be aware of the adoptee's sense of loss and recognize that more is needed than simply their love when responding to this pain, then disenfranchised grief and its behavioral consequences need not be a defining part of the adoptee's narrative.

Intimacy. Intimacy, that sense of comfort being physically and emotionally close to others, is thought to mark adoptees' narrative identities. Having been separated from the woman who carried the adoptee to term, placed with strangers either directly into an adoptive home or following multiple placements and having had less than optimal support in the process of grieving one's losses, the end result of this history would be a marked deficiency in intimate relationships. To open oneself up to others would be to make oneself vulnerable again to loss or trauma. To trust that people who are close will provide reliable and safe caretaking would mean that one became less self-protective and hence, less prepared for disappointment. Better to stay at a safe distance where intimacy may suffer, but one feels protected from personal intrusion and psychological assault. It is, therefore, quite reassuring that Borders, Penny and Portnoy (2000), in a study of adult adoptees found that their intimacy concerns were no different than their friends who had not been adopted. Perhaps this finding is reflective of the fact that the adults in this study were primarily adopted at birth and, thus, had not had the experience of being raised by multiple caretakers. For those who have been adopted in the last two decades, the story may be very different. The demographics of adoption (Daly & Sobol, 1993) have shifted from infant to older child placements. This latter group has experienced many settings with various levels of personal care. It is this group whose lack of comfort with intimacy should be characterized as a normal response to an abnormal situation. Without the early experience of close, reliable, and loving relationships, it is difficult to imagine their response being otherwise. This is not to say that all adoptees who were adopted after many placements or were older at placement are marked by a lack of comfort with intimacy. It is only to imply that challenges in this domain are to be reasonably expected.

Mastery and control. Although the word adoptee is a noun, representing a particular family status, it is often experienced as a passive verb. It is a state in which things happen to one, rather than a status defined by directed action and control. Adoptees usually came into families as the result of decisions made by social workers, judges, attorneys, and birth, foster and adoptive parents. Consent was not an option for young adoptees and was rarely given freely by older ones. One ended up with the status of an adoptee because of the needs and choices of others. Adoptees, thus, often entered into their role with the underlying assumption that this was not of their doing. Too often I have heard social workers complain that an older potential adoptee was being unreasonable when resistance to an adoption plan was displayed. Rarely is this seen as an expression of a need to feel control over one's destiny. On the other hand, there is little to match the joyful choice, freely made by a child who sees a possible placement as a means of being freed from the endless circle of foster care and group homes. The difference between these two scenarios is found, of course, in the sense of control experienced by the child.

How is control manifested for adoptees who are challenged by a lack of control. For some, there is a seeking out of all means possible for being the best child ever. This exercise in control has several outcomes: one acts in a way that always remains within the parental parameters of acceptableness, thus making the child valued by the parents; spontaneity is sacrificed to maintain this control; and as circles of interaction widen beyond the immediate family, the adoptee carries this need for control into other domains of experience, which simply intensifies the challenge of always being in control.

Control is also exercised in a paradoxical fashion, by demonstrating what seemingly appears to be a complete lack of control. The child's behavior is marked by spontaneity, risk taking and impulsiveness, or so it would seem to the casual observer. A more careful look will reveal a child whose control is manifested in decisions not to follow the rules, to act in a manner that is seen by others as contrary to the limits set by caretakers. Some adoptees use what they know of their birth parents' history as a template for how they will demonstrate control in their life. If the birth parent was a risk taker, they will also be one. If the birth parent became pregnant, then they will exercise control by following in their footsteps. This may not be an adaptive choice but it serves one's need for mastery in the world.

For adoptive parents, finding a means of being responsible parents and at the same time, allowing their children to develop a sense of control is, indeed, a challenge. However, simply being aware of adoptees' need for control is an important first step in helping them to make safe and self-enhancing choices. Adoptive parents are often overly solicitous of their children's safety and, hence, go out of their way to keep them out of harm's way. The paradox is that doing so in an overly controlling manner, leads the adoptee to strive more vigorously for personal control. The narrative result of this encounter is a story of anger and resentment for restrictions placed upon the exercise of control, feelings of incompetence as a result of not having had an opportunity to make choices that would have proven to be good ones, and lowered feelings of self worth brought on by not being able to tie positive outcomes to personal initiative. On the other hand, when parents recognize that their children's need for control is not a rejection of their parental authority as much as it is an expression of a need to demonstrate competence in the world, then the narrative result is a sense of efficaciousness and self worth permeating many domains of experience.

I once heard an adult adoptee say at the age of 38 that he realized his parents were growing older and he needed to express what it meant to him to having been adopted by them. He described a highly charged, emotionally positive exchange as he portrayed their journey together over the rocky road of development. In essence, he was saying to them, "I am finally as a 38 year old able to adopt you as my parents." This act represented a new chapter in his narrative identity of adoption. His story is unique, but in so many ways provided a strong, positive narrative theme of mastery and control. After all, he was the one now choosing to pursue the adoption of the parents, not the other way round as adoption is traditionally conceived. If only all adoptees were able to incorporate this into their own identity narratives.

Mattering[15]. In 1890, William James, one of the forefathers of modern Psychology, wrote: "We all have an innate propensity to get ourselves noticed...by our kind. No more fiendish punishment could be devised ...than that one should be turned loose in society and remain absolutely unnoticed by all the members thereof" (p. 293). Almost 100 years later, Rosenberg and MuCullough (1981) formalized James's observation by defining the construct of mattering as the perception that we are a significant part of the experience of others who occupy our social space. In other words, we sense that we matter to others who we are important to us. They are interested

---

15 Mattering is not one of the core themes articulated by Silverstein and Rozsia (2001). However, I believe that it is one that should be included as it is a fundamental theme in the narratives of adoptees, birth parents and adoptive parents alike. I am grateful for discussions I have had with Sheila Marshall at the University of British Columbia, who introduced me to the concept and Sharon Rozsia and the staff of the Kinship Center in California who have assisted me in fleshing out this eighth core value in adoption.

in us, what we do, how we feel, what we say, and the state of our overall being. In contrast, if others do not care what we feel, think, say and do, if our existence is of no relevance to them, then it is as if we do not exist. For all intents and purposes, in such settings, we perceive ourselves to be irrelevant to others, to be of no consequence.

Elliot, Kao and Grant, (2004), identified two kinds of inter-personal mattering. The first was that we perceive that others are aware that we exist. While this form of mattering clearly has implications on a societal level for establishing social connected-ness, on the micro level of analysis, mattering is more than simply recognition of one's presence. It is the perception that one is not only seen to be present but also as occupying a valued social role. If we perceive that others do not value our presence, we become a non-person, one who clearly does not matter to others.

The second super ordinate construct offered by Elliot et al., (2004) is relationship. We sense that we matter to others if their interests and concerns are directed to us. When we perceive that significant others care about our wellbeing, are willing to offer resources to help us match our goals and take pride not only in what we are able to accomplish, but more importantly, that we are in meaningful relationship with them, then we perceive ourselves to truly matter to others. We view their investment in what hap-pens to us as a reflection of the fact that we make a difference to them, that we are important to them.

Since mattering is defined as grounded within a relationship with another, it is, therefore, apparent that mattering should be thought of as bi-directional. Thus, we also have a sense of mat-tering when we perceive ourselves as having an effect on others. This focus of mattering involves noting others' reliance as they look to us to help them satisfy their own needs or goals. However, in order to achieve this sense of mattering, one must not feel used or exploited. This can happen when others welcome our accom-plishments as a reflection of themselves, while, at the same time, ignoring our sense of wellbeing.

According to Elliot et al., (2004), mattering is increased if one feels that one has been uniquely chosen to be the recipient of others' attention or selected as the source of the actualization of others' needs. From such a viewpoint, a person with a strong sense of mattering perceives herself to possess special attributes that are valued by the other in the relationship.

The literature on mattering is just in its infancy. Unfortunately, we have yet to see research on the role of mattering for adoptees. What we do know from developmental studies is that the more adolescents feel they matter to their parents, the less they will display both externalizing and internalizing difficulties (Schenck, Braver, Wolchik, Saenz, Cookston, & Fabricius, 2009). Dixon, Scheidegger, and McWhirter (2009) found parallel results: adolescent anxiety and depression were negatively related to mattering to parents. Rosenberg (1989) reported that those adolescents who received positive support for their academic achievement had the highest levels of self esteem, presumably an index of the degree their work mattered to their parents. When comparing those who had parents who acted in a punitive fashion for inadequate academic achievement with those who received no feedback for academic shortcomings, the former group reported higher levels of self-esteem than did those who were ignored by their parents. Presumably, feedback, even when it is negative is perceived as providing evidence of mattering.

Marshall (2001) also found relatively strong relationships between possessing a sense that one mattered to parents and other variables reflecting family relationships. For example, the more high school students and university undergraduates felt they mattered to their parents, the greater their sense of family cohesion and social support. Furthermore, mattering to others was also positively related to having a strong sense of purpose in life.

In so many ways, mattering lies at the heart of the experience of adoption. At the front end of adoption, how does the woman about to give birth matter to potential adoptive parents? Is she seen to be nothing more than an incubator of the adopting parents' child or is she viewed as a person who is valued for her courage to bring a fetus to term in the face of societal approbation; a person whose fear, uncertainty, and sense of abandonment are of genuine concern to those who are about to claim her child as their own. And how will she matter to the adoptive parents in the years following placement? Will she be nothing more a source of threat to the integrity of the adoptive family, that morally loose individual whose genetic influence must be compensated for by superior parenting? Or will she be seen as a partner, even a distant one, who shares in the development and well being of the adoptee? Will the adoptive parents let her know that she matters to them, that they will forever be grateful that she brought a child into their lives, that they worry whether she has found a way to live with the circumstance that led her child to adoption?

Adoptive parents, who invite the birth family into their lives, create a bi-directional atmosphere of mattering. Birth parents find that they matter not only to the adoptee but also to those who raise the child. Adoptive parents learn that they matter to the parents who brought the child into the world. Adoptees, if they have the opportunity to observe this bidirectional mattering between their two sets of parents, will be at an advantage in being able to incorporate mattering into their narrative of adoptive identity.

How is mattering expressed within the adoptive parent-child relationship? It is hard to imagine parents, adoptive or not, who can claim satisfaction in the role of parent without having a sense that they matter to their children as a valued source of support, nurturance, affection and direction. Parents wait for that spontaneous hug or a word of acknowledgement of their role in helping the child meet his goals. To matter to a child is to receive certification of authenticity as a parent. While this comes relatively easily for those who have adopted a healthy infant from birth, it is likely not the case for those who have adopted an older child, one with a multitude of placements or a history of trauma and abuse. In such circumstances, the child has little expectation that the parent will prove to be a reliable or trustworthy source of nurturance. Hence, in that period of testing the limits of the relationship, parents receive little feedback that they matter to their child. In many ways, this experience parallels that of parents of children with autism who find themselves fulfilling their parental responsibilities with greatly reduced, positive feedback from their children. Some adoptive parents, often with professional support, are able to bridge this period until their children are able to provide feedback that they matter. However, others resort to an attachment-based explanation of their relationship with their children, claiming that the child has failed to securely connect to them. Interestingly, this explanation is rarely accompanied by a recognition that the parents may have failed to form a strong, positive relationship with the child.

I believe that this flight to attachment disorder fails to capture the essence of the problem: the parents have yet to matter to the child and the child has yet to matter to the parents. How do we cross this abyss? The task is not an easy one. Adoptive parents must first recognize that the child is currently acting in a manner totally consistent with her developmental history. With this in mind, when the child does not expect to matter to adults, it falls to the adoptive parents to offer positive regard to the child without consideration of the acceptability of the child's behavior. By doing so, they create an emotionally, educative experience unlike any other the child has had before. The message to the child is clear: You and your wellbeing matter to me regardless of how you act. I am not saying that parents should abrogate their responsibilities to insure their children's safety and socialization, for example, by failing to set appropriate behavioral limits when necessary. What they must do, however, is send the message, less through words than action and affect, that the child, no matter what happens, is a valued person whose existence truly matters to them. Touch, smile, laughter, gentle reprimand, guidance, sacrifice without martyrdom all say to the child, "you matter to me." Even punishment when delivered without denigration or violence says "You matter to me so much that I must place limits on some of your behaviors." If these messages are delivered clearly and without exploitation, then one opens up the possibility that the child will experience the parents as adults to whom he feels he matters.

The fundamental question that every adoptee must face at some point in development is: "Why did I not matter enough to my birth mother for her to have raised me instead of giving me up for adoption?" No amount of discussion with an adoptive parent will take away the possibility of this question being asked. It emerges naturally out of the circumstance of starting with one family and ending up with another. When the placement was a voluntary one, adoptive parents are typically instructed to tell their children that their birth mothers loved them but she did not have the means to care for them. Hence, their placement into an adoptive home was a gift of love and concern to provide for their wellbeing. If the placement was involuntary, the story often centers on the birth mother's inability to care for the child during the period prior to becoming a member of the adoptive family. These story may serve the needs of the child in the early telling of the adoption placement narrative, but with the child's development, they fail to directly address the core issue: What was it about me that made me not matter enough for her to keep me? Unfortunately, there are adoptive parents who encourage the child to hold on to this level of understanding, in that they use it as a means of establishing themselves as legitimate parents who by their actions demonstrate their sense of mattering to the child. Paradoxically, this rarely leads to a shift in the adoptee's sense of negative mattering.

As children grow older, they develop the cognitive capacity to take others' perspectives into consideration and to evaluate behavior in context. Now, the placement narrative may be understood as a story in which the birth mother did not matter much to others. As a result, they withheld the support necessary for her to be able to parent the child. Thus, she had no other choice than to give up trying to be a parent, and to let the child go to another family. Such a story shifts the focus from the lack of worth of the child and places it empathetically on the lack of worth experienced by the birth parent. This rendition of the placement narrative opens up the possibility for the adoptee to diminish the anger attached to the historical fact of moving from family to family. This narrative of forgiveness in turn, lessens the emotional salience of being adopted, and allows for a sense of mattering to all of the important adults in one's life, both in the birth and adoptive families.

Issues of mattering do not end, however, with the telling of the placement story. There are other times in the lives of adoptees when they feel that they do not matter to their adoptive parents. If parents fail to attend to their children's grief over the loss of the birth family or the loss of a self altered by the fact of adoption, what we have referred to as disenfranchised grief, then they are sending a clear message that the feelings of the adoptee do not matter as they do not merit parental attention.

Another form of not mattering occurs when parents fail to recognize that their own interests, skills and aptitudes are not necessarily ones that come easily to their adopted children. A majority of adoptive parents have received a higher education (Daly & Sobol, 1993). Adoptees as a group, however, display less educational success than their adoptive parents. Thus, if they are chastised for a lack of school success, this sends a message to the children that their efforts are not valued as they did not result in acceptable school performance.

Some adoptees may go out of their way to engage in negative or self-harming behaviors in an attempt to increase parental mattering. Perceiving that their socially acceptable behavior does not matter to their parents, this group of adoptees may turn to more extreme behaviors in an attempt to get their parents to acknowledge that the well being of the adoptee actually matters to them. Whether it is the parent's distancing from the child or the child's failure to recognize the parent's mattering communications, the end result is a play for feeling that one matters in the world, even if one needs to break the rules to do so.

Although there are no statistics indicating how many adoptees find themselves in circumstances similar to the ones that the birth family dealt with prior to placement, it is not uncommon for adolescent adoptees to become pregnant. Some have suggested that adoptee teen pregnancy is a way of reliving the circumstance of birth and placement in an attempt to render the early circumstances of one's life in a clearer perspective. I suspect that for many adoptees, becoming pregnant is a means for dealing with the existential struggle of feeling that you matter to no one, particularly, adoptive parents. Pregnancy, therefore, is a means of bringing a person into the world who will need the teen mom and who will provide evidence that she truly matters to someone. Thus, pregnancy and birth is more than simply replicating the past. It is a means of addressing a core theme of adoption: will I matter to someone in my life?

Trust[16]. If possessing a sense of mattering underscores the valence of the connections we perceive ourselves to have with others, then trust is the consequence of living such relationships. To believe that we matter to others means that they can be trusted to be attuned to our needs and to respond in a manner that does not leave us questioning the safety of our relationships. However, trust is not just a sense of security in our interactions with significant others. We also develop a sense of self that entails accepting that our bodies and our very psychological being will be trustworthy to meet our needs; that they will able to respond to the challenges that leave us feeling that we have a sense of worth. These themes are played out differently for each of the major players in the adoption constellation.

For adoptive parents, the first violation of trust that marks their narrative involves fertility status. Most adults conduct their sexual relationships with the expectation that they are fertile beings.

---

16   Trust, like mattering, is not one of the original core issues that Silverstein and Rozsia (2001) articulated.

Therefore, the realization that either one or both members of the couple may be infertile comes not only as a disappointment, but also as a lack of trust that one's body will function effectively as one had always thought it would. For many infertile individuals, this realization is not a slowly evolving expectation grounded in wider medical concerns. Rather, it is experienced as a relatively rapid violation of a sense of self that has been part of one's sexual identity prior to trying to become pregnant. Left with a sense that one's very physical being is flawed opens up the possibility that one may also lack the means to meet other developmental life challenges.

Once having acknowledged that one's body cannot be trusted, some couples and individuals move on to consider the possibility of adoption as an alternative means of family formation (Daly, 1988). As part of the process of establishing an adoptive family, the adopters must put themselves into the hands of a social worker who is charged with determining whether the family has the resources, both psychological and material, for becoming adoptive parents. Potential adopters typically try to portray their best image, trusting that the social worker will see their inherent worth as adoption candidates. If they pass this hurdle, trust next emerges when they are presented with the life scenarios of children who are available for adoption. Do they have a true and full account of the child's background? Was the child exposed prenatally to harmful substances? Was the child abused? Will this child be a good match for them? Will the birth parent withdraw the consent to the adoption prior to finalization? All of these questions are based on the assumption that each of the parties to the adoption is trustworthy. If this proves not to be the case, again, a lack of trust will permeate the adoption narrative.

Today, children who are available for adoption are quite different than those of even a decade ago. Many are older, with challenging backgrounds of exposure to toxins in utero, post-natal abuse and neglect, as well as a history of multiple caretakers. It is, therefore, not surprising that adoptive parents do not always trust themselves to be able to meet the child's needs. Furthermore, given that many children from abusive backgrounds use physical aggression and emotional outbursts as means of coping with life's frustrations, is it any wonder that parents may not trust that they are safe when the child has lost control, nor do they trust that they can be loving and appropriate parents for such children.

Finally, adoptive parents rarely trust the positive message of open relationships between adoptive and birth families. Having seen themselves as the rescuers and entitled parents of the child, they do not trust that the birth family, if given access to the child, will act with the best interests of the child in mind. All of this is said in the face of 30 years of research that proves otherwise. Nevertheless, for many adoptive parents, birth family contact, whether as part of a prior agreement or stemming from a search, is viewed as a risky matter, as "the other" is deemed to be untrustworthy. Such thinking is part of a long string of events that have challenged the adoptive parents' sense of trust.

Birth parents also experience trust as a central theme in their adoptive narrative. The first violation of trust begins with the realization of their pregnancy. Can significant others in the life of the mother, her parents and the father of the child, be trusted to stand with her as decisions are being made or will they abandon her to her own resources without emotional or monetary means of support? If the pregnant woman seeks out information about her options, can she trust that her needs and the needs of her child will be considered or will the counselor, social worker or physician act only as the procurer of a child for those willing to pay the cost of such a service?

Today, openness marks most infant placements and a growing number of older child adoptions (Daly & Sobol, 1993). Many promises are made prior to placement, outlining the parameters of contact between birth and adoptive families. Sometimes these agreements are written. Often they are simply oral promises. In either case, in most jurisdictions these agreements have no legal status once the legal relinquishment process has been completed.

Hence, for birth parents, the question that remains is whether the adoptive parents can be trusted to fulfill the agreement. If it was only entered into by the adoptive parents as a means of gaining access to the child, then birth parents' sense of trust will be truly violated, particularly as the courts will rarely grant them recourse when the provisions of an openness agreement have been ignored.

A variation on this theme is prominent in the experience of birth mothers who are now in their fifties and sixties[17]. Many were promised that if they agreed not to contest the adoption but instead "voluntarily gave up their child," then the child, as an adult, would be given identifying information that could lead to reunion. Clearly, social workers had no authority to speak about how the law would apply in the future. It is a sad reality that most jurisdictions in North America still do not allow easy access to identifying information. The consequence is a blatant violation of trust. Birth parents gave consent to the adoption based on false information. They now find themselves without legal recourse to rectify the situation. Having been misled, many birth parents carry a sense of historical helplessness, based upon circumstances they could not have predicted. This is a true violation of the trust that professional relationships are supposed to safeguard: the best interests of *all* parties to the adoption.

Trust is also a core issue for adoptees. The historical reality for adoptees is that they were born into a family that did not maintain a continuing, direct familial role with them. Furthermore, those children who have come to adoption through the child welfare system typically have experienced multiple placements with foster parents, group homes and, in some cases, other adoptive families. The result, for these adoptees, is a belief that their current adoption placement also will not be permanent, particularly if any misstep or challenge to the authority of the family is met with

---

17 This theme is often heard at legislative hearings held to consider the possibility of changing the law to allow for the exchange of identifying information between adult adoptees and their birth kin.

a threat of exile from the home. Thus, children learn that close relationships are untrustworthy. Unconditional acceptance of the bonds between others cannot be relied upon. When affection and expressions of mattering are offered in a conditional manner, and not as spontaneous expressions of the depth and enduring nature of the parent-child relationship, then adoptees are left feeling that emotional relationships are not to be trusted.

Sometimes professionals and parents, when faced with a child who does not trust them, refer to such a child as having an attachment disorder. However, why should the child be pathologized? After all, given the pre placement history, the child is acting normally in an untrustworthy situation. To act otherwise would necessitate denying the reality of that history. Thus, if we wish to see adoptive parent-child relationships thrive, it would be better to focus attention on generating trusting patterns of interaction rather than changing the child's so called "pathological behavior." One place to start would be to identify interactional patterns between parent and child when the child is expressing an historical sense of mistrust in others. This is not the time for discipline. It is the time for understanding and unconditional regard, the purpose of which is to convey to the child that no matter what the behavior of the child, the relationship will endure. This message is best conveyed not through words that cannot be trusted, but through actions. Children need to learn new ways to respond in the face of situations deemed to be untrustworthy. However, to do so, they need parental partners who also must meet the challenge of changing their own ways when faced with the message that their children do not trust them to be fully present in the relationship. Taking such a perspective requires that the parents assume a greater degree of responsibility for the change process. They must learn to calibrate their dance steps to their children's rhythms. Therapy designed to alter children when parents remain poor dance partners is doomed to little effect.

There are other trust issues for adoptees. One of the most important relates to whether they can trust that the narrative facts they have been given about their adoption journey are true. Most adoptive parents are uncomfortable first sharing any part of the adoption story, let alone the most emotionally laden aspects of the child's history. Nevertheless, it is a story that must be told. This is why it is always best to begin telling the story as early as possible. For parents of very young children, there is an advantage in telling a version of the story well before the child has the cognitive competence to understand the full import of the facts. This will give parents a chance to desensitize themselves to the sharing of information. As the child grows older, the story must be repeated several times, always with a rendition that reflects the child's growing cognitive and emotional maturity and a commitment to be as truthful as possible. By the age of 12, there is rarely a reason why the child should not be in possession of all the facts, no matter how uncomfortable they might be. Better to learn them from their parents than from others, a situation that often occurs when parents are reluctant to share information with their children.

One final word about trust and narrative truth: It is a sad reality that many adoptees who reconnect with birth kin learn that the story their adoptive parents told them or the story their adoptive parents were given by social workers was either false or missing significant information. Many adoptees construe this flawed narrative as representing a parental belief that the adoptee lacked the wherewithal to manage such sensitive information. Sadly, this adds a negative tinge to one's narrative identity as the adoptee is forced to conclude that others see him as a person who cannot be trusted with the truth.

Often I have heard adoptees recall that although they often thought of their birth kin with longing, sadness and sometimes anger, they did not trust their adoptive parents enough to share these feelings. They feared the parents would see this interest in birth kin as a betrayal of the commitment that that had been made to incorporate them into the family. However, is such sharing of difficulty emotional material not the very test of the strength of a relationship: that we can be wholly present with another when pain and loss are being experienced. It is easy to be with others when joy and contentment are the norm. Trust, however, is more often built when relationships are under stress, when there are no easy or comfortable means of addressing pain other than to be fully with the other. Adoptees will not trust their adoptive parents if the parents flee from strong feelings. Parents must model mature adaptive strategies with their children particularly in such difficult moments, for it is here that children will learn to feel an enduring sense of security.

The final trust theme focuses on how the adoptive parents respond to their child's motivation to search and the realities of reunion and reconnection with birth kin. These journeys are not a betrayal of the adoptive parents nor are they a rejection of all that has transpired over the course of the adoption. Reconnection is an expansion of a sense of self. It is a coming to terms with the historical realities of one's life. It is finding out who you are as a genetic being, whom you look like, who shares your aptitudes, proclivities, and temperament. It is a fleshing out of a narrative of self that was missing from the first chapter of one's life. It is the repair of a deficient narrative. If adoptive parents trust and support their children on this journey to a full sense of self, they will end up enhancing their relationships like little else can (Sobol & Cardiff, 1983). No relationship can thrive and grow stronger without such trust.

Conclusion:

Identity, that iterative process of defining and redefining a sense of who we are, even as we perceive that our core being persists over time, is grounded in the stories we tell about ourselves and our history. Consciously, we strive for historical truth but in the end, what we end up with is narrative truth, a truth that is shaped in the service of making sense of our lives (Spence 1982). Structural and process factors such as openness of communication, parental gate keeping of information, legislative access to historical documents and community attitudes and beliefs all shape the wide outline of adoptees' stories. Core issues of loss, rejection, grief, intimacy, shame and guilt, mastery and control, mattering and trust provide the core themes of the narratives. For some adoptees, the identity story is a positive one. For others, it is a heavy burden that serves as a template for all of life's experiences. The question that we must ask is whether this need be the case, or whether there are better ways for us to meet the challenges that adoption brings us.

CHAPTER 5

EXPANDING THE CHOICES

*I am not what happened to me. I am
what I choose to become. Carl Jung*

Much of modern day adoption is premised on the historical realities of times past. Today we practice family formation through adoption as if we are still trying to co-manage the moral reputation of young, single pregnant women and older, infertile adopting couples. Behind our laws lies the assumption of stigmatized identities in need of protection and repair. Legislation is framed to hide the shame of pregnancy and its resolution. We strive to make the adopting parents into the only parents the child has ever had. Birth records are modified to create a revisionist history, and efforts to reunite birth families and adoptees are thwarted at every turn.

And yet, if we reflect on the current world of adoption, what we see is a very different picture. The stigma of extra marital pregnancy has been greatly diminished as out of wedlock child bearing becomes more acceptable in the Western world (Sobol & Daly, 1994). Services for keeping a child, completing an education and providing subsidized housing are available in many jurisdictions. We no longer expect pregnant teens to hide away from public scrutiny. This change is reflected in the demographics of adoption as the proportion of live births available for adoption continues to diminish (Sobol & Daly, 1994). Given this shift in the nature of the context in which adoption takes place, the time has come for us to expand the options available to children in need of families. Are we only left with the choice of foster care or adoption? Must parents who have brought a child into the world be permanently separated legally and relationally from their children? Must we accept what Paul Watzlawick (1974) called the illusion of alternatives: choose A or not A, when, in fact, there is another viable alternative, B? In the following pages, some of these alternatives will be described.

Guardianship

Over the past half-century, we have seen a major shift in the demographics of adoption (Sobol & Daly, 1994). No longer do healthy Caucasian infants, without identified physical or intellectual needs, make up the majority of those being placed. Today, the majority of adoptions are of older children, of mixed ethnic heritage who have experienced a variety of pre and postnatal challenges. It is no longer common practice to split up sibling groups, and if we accept the words of those who place children, no child should ever be considered unadoptable. In this new world of possibilities, where adoption is seen as serving both the best interests of the child[18] and the state (by removing the state's financial responsibilities while the child is on the foster care roster), one often hears social workers complaining that the adoption is being delayed by older children's refusal to consent to an adoption. As one social worker put it to me, "...the kid likes the freedom of a group home and didn't want to live under the rules of the adoptive one. He just refused to be adopted." This social worker was defining what he thought was

---

18   The phrase, best interests of the child, appears often in the adoption literature but rarely is it ever defined. Typically, it is used to indicate that a decision is being made that is thought to improve the life circumstances of the child. Rarely however, do we ask whether the decision was experienced by the child as a positive one. In fact, Guggenheim (2005) has suggested that best interests are nothing more than a reflection of a family court judge's values and attitudes, the desire of state officials to rid themselves of the responsibilities for the child or the substituting of adopting parents' interests for those of the child. I believe the phrase is used sincerely to mirror the needs of the child. Unfortunately, this usage is rarely accompanied by an examination of the intrusion of other competing expressions of interest.

best for the child. He saw his responsibility being to talk the child into agreeing to the adoption. From his perspective, the child simply failed to subscribe to a more long-term view. We think of adoptive homes as being superior to other living arrangements for these children. By framing this course of action in positive terms, we ignore the possibility that many older adoptees do not want to loose their name and all that it contributes to their sense of who they are. They have walked too far in the shoes of one identity to easily shed it for another.

What possibilities are available for children who do not believe that adoption is in their best interests? Clearly long term group home experience is not the answer as children raised in such settings are at a disadvantage as they age out of the system, finding themselves alone in the world. This cohort is more prone to be unemployed, to get into trouble with the law and to become substance abusers (Triseliotis & Hill, 1990). An alternative is to consider long term foster care within a single placement, where the foster parents are granted guardianship of the child. In offering such a recommendation, I am not considering placements in settings where the responsible adults use foster care as an income generator and who have no expectations or desire to make a long-term commitment to a child. Rather, we should be cultivating a cohort of foster parent guardians from the ranks of those wishing to adopt a child and are willing to bring an older, and service-weary child into their home on a permanent basis. The family would be expected to take on all of the responsibilities of an adoptive one, but would not carry the legal mantel of adoption as it may fail to meet the desires or consent of the child.

It is anticipated that potential adoptive parents will object to such an arrangement as it would be seen to be second best. The child would not carry their name. They would not have the authority of legal, permanent parents nor would they be granted the status of authenticity of adoptive parents. However, guardianship, particularly in the face of the child's rejection of adoption, paradoxically carries with it the possibility of child and parent growing closer than would be possible in a forced adoption circumstance. Not pressuring the child into offering consent, gives the child a sense of mastery and control. He enters the guardianship setting without the resentment that accompanies a loss of personal agency. As Watzlawick, et al (1974) have clinically demonstrated, by asking less of someone, the person is in a position of giving more without being pushed into a corner to do so.

Guardianship not only takes the pressure off the child but also those who have agreed to take legal responsibility for the child. It redefines the situation as one in which each participant is freely able to enter the relationship and not be tied to the potential stigma of failing to make it work. I believe that many prospective adoptive parents would consider the option of adopting an older child or a sibling group if they were first offered the possibility of legal guardianship. Such a status serves a bridging function as child or children and the guardian grow to accept each other and the roles and responsibilities that each brings to the relationship. It allows for a trial period of growth while beginning to create a history of interaction. The message to the child is that this is a safe and good place to be, and it allows the guardian to feel that a move towards future permanence is desirable and appropriate. Some families may never reach the point of conversion from guardianship to adoption. This should not be the mark of success. What long term guardianship is directed towards is the development of reciprocal respect and affectionate commitment to each other. If this is the result, then whether an adoption is the consequence is simply a matter of personal choice, a means of operationalizing what the relationship means to children and parent. It is not the reason for the relationship. It becomes the consequence of it.

Adopting a Parent and Child Together

Silverstein and Rozsia (2002) have argued that loss is a defining theme in the lives of those involved with adoption. Birth parents have lost their children, adoptive parents have lost the opportunity to raise a child of their own DNA and adoptees have lost both a relationship with their birth kin and a self that would have been if they had been raised within their birth family. Each of these players and others within the adoptive constellation must find accommodations to this loss. The loss is rarely experienced as a one-time event but resurfaces with each new developmental transition.

What would happen, however, if the loss were not an inevitable outcome of an unplanned pregnancy? What would happen if the child and parent were not separated but instead were adopted together by a family? Is this an outrageous possibility or could we conceive of a circumstance where two generations came under the wing of a new family? To answer this question we must draw upon several themes.

It is a sad reality that parents whose children end up being placed for adoption rarely come from backgrounds where they can draw upon resource-rich environments. Most of these parents are poor, have less education than the norm, have had a history of involvement with support services and cannot look to their own families of origin or partner for support in the continuance of a parenting role. What we are left with is a situation where resource-rich individuals adopt the children of resource poor ones. Given that power is tied to resources and choice is only available to those who can exercise their power, it is difficult for parents whose children are placed to see adoption as being anything other than the exploitation of power. This perception is held, even in the face of evidence that the child will be granted entrance into a world of enhanced possibilities that the parent could not possibly provide. This is a harsh painting of the picture of adoption, but it is one that is rarely acknowledged. Poor people do not adopt the children of the wealthy. The relationship is always in the opposite direction.

Would parents ever consider being adopted along with their child, hence, creating an adoptive family where the adopter has the simultaneous dual roles of adoptive parent and grandparent?

I believe this is a possibility. It is now a truism that parents whose legal rights to their child are relinquished do not "forget about the child and get on with their lives" (Winkler & Von Keppel, 1986). They carry that child in their hearts, sometimes burying her deeply and rarely grieving openly. The most we can say is that when the child was placed, if the parent felt a sense of personal agency in the decision making process, then the pain of placement is attenuated to some degree. Given that many parents "gave up" fighting the overpowering forces pushing them to place the child, and given that many were abandoned by their birth kin and partner, adoption by a couple who are willing to bring them into another family could be seen as a viable response to difficult circumstances.

Many adopting couples are older than consanguineous parents at the point when adopted children come into their homes. In adopting the parent and the child, the parent would in all likelihood be the same age as the adopting couple's own birth children if the couple had not faced infertility. Thus, age of the parent does not necessarily provide an insurmountable barrier to a relationship. Blended families often face a parallel situation. Some of the children are older adolescents or young adults and the new spouse must establish a relationship with them.

Let us consider the adoptive grandchild and the adopting grandparent? Many grandparents report that their relationship with their grandchildren was easier and less stressful than their relationship with their own children. This being the case, we would expect a similar situation to arise in a bigenerational adoption. Grandparents offer emotional support to the parent in the management of the child, respite care when the parent needs to temporally separate from the child and resources of a more material nature to supplement those provided by the parent.

Perhaps the biggest challenge to a bigenerational adoption is defining and maintaining effective boundaries around parenting. If the boundaries were too porous, then parent and adoptive grandparent would be continually in conflict. If the boundaries were too rigid, there would be no interactive benefit within the relationship. Thus, clarity, specificity and respect must mark the communications between the parties as they sort out who is responsible for what in the relationship. If families sort this out, then the adopting family can be a valuable resource to the parent and child.

However, a caveat is necessary. Bigenerational adoption is not being recommended as an alternative to child adoption, if it is undertaken with the intent to hide the genetic relationship of the mother and her child. To pass the mother off as an older sister will forever distort the relationships between the parties to the adoption. By adopting the parent, the adoptive grandparents must explicitly recognize that they are bringing a parent-child dyad under the protective wing of their family. This family relationship is a complex one which will need to be renegotiated several times over the lifetime of the family. As long as we see this as the challenge, and not an impediment to the adoption, this new form of family formation may prove to be a viable alternative to child adoption and one that preserves the parent-child relationship.

Second Chances

When we think of adoptive families, we think of them as "forever families." However, like non-adoptive families, this is not always the case. Sometimes children are removed from the adoptive family prior to the finalization of the adoption and placed either into foster care or another adoptive family. This is referred to as adoption disruption. The second form of family breakup is called adoption dissolution and occurs when the child is legally severed from the adoptive family and is placed into foster care or with another adoptive family. Rates for these two situations vary by time and place. Festinger (2001) reported that, excluding older child adoptions, between 9 and 15% of children are removed from their first adoptive family prior to the finalization of the adoption. For older children, the disruption rate jumps up to 25%. Barth, Gibbs, and Siebenaler (2001) found comparable rates of between

10% and 16% for children over three years of age. In a study of adolescent placements where the child was between 12 and 17, Berry and Barth (1990) reported that 24% ended in disruption.

It is not surprising to find that the longer a child is in an adoptive home, the lower the rate of dissolution. After all, the length of time to dissolution should reflect the degree of strength individual families would have to cope with the stress of a challenging adoption. Thus, Festinger (2002) found a dissolution rate of 3.3%, four years after finalization and McDonald, Propp, & Murphy, (2001) reported a similar rate of 3%, a year and a half to two years after the legal aspects of the adoption had been completed.

What happens to these children following dissolution? Typically, they return to the system they were in, prior to the adoption. Placed in a foster or group home, a search begins for a new family and hopefully, support services that would assist in the adjustment of the child. What is missing from this scenario is a current assessment of the life circumstances of the birth family and their kin. Rarely is consideration given to the question as to whether either or both of the birth parents might be willing or are able to retake an active parenting role. We never ask whether the circumstances that led to placement have now changed. We do not seek out information about the present life skills of the birth parent. We ignore the extended kin, and never assume that they will be able to raise the child or provide support for the birth parent to do so. What is being suggested is that when dissolution occurs, it is an ethical responsibility of adoption placement workers to consider the possibility of the birth parents reestablishing an active parenting role.

Why do I say it is an ethical responsibility? The reason lies in the fact that at its heart, adoption is a response to loss. As such, the loss, being a historical and psychological reality, can never disappear as long as parent and child are not in an active relationship. If the parent is unable or unwilling to be in this role, then adoption becomes a viable substitute. However, until we can establish that it is unsafe for the child to be under the responsibility of the parent, this must be considered our first line of action. We often hear the phrase "the best interests of the child" as the guiding principle of decision making, yet we ignore the possibility of placing the child back with birth kin when there is justification for doing so. It is time to switch our mode of thinking on this matter, and to bring birth parents to the foreground after dissolution, with the intent of allowing them to shed the label of birth parent and again retake the mantel of parent.

In Western society, individuals whose parental rights have been transferred to others are considered to have broken a natural law of consanguineous family formation, regardless of whether they bore responsibility for the severing of the tie, or whether they accepted it. Thus, if their child were to become available for reconnection, we morally reject this possibility, since having considered them to have once sinned, we treat them as if there is no possibility of future redemption. It is time to take adoption out of this moral arena, and place it back into the domain of relationship, recognizing that choice is not always freely given and that circumstances can change.

Embryo adoption.

To fully understand adoption, it is necessary to be aware of how it is grounded in a wider cultural discourse about family formation. Using the systemic orientation of the adoption constellation as our foundation, it readily becomes apparent that attitudes and practices in adoption will affect other forms of creating families.

Over the course of the past two decades, the public adoption of healthy young infants has declined significantly. With changing attitudes towards single parenthood and increased supports for young mothers, few infants are being brought forward today for adoption. Where are infertile couples and individuals to turn then? The answer lies in the burgeoning field of assisted reproductive technology. Where once it was the stuff of science fiction, today the myriad of procedures for creating an embryo seems to know no bounds. Gamete donations of eggs or sperm are common occurrences, in vitro fertilization is a fully accepted medical procedure and the implanting of an embryo, genetically unrelated to a receiving couple, into the womb of a surrogate mother, no longer seems out of the ordinary. This new age of reproductive possibilities brings with it an assortment of ethical and practical concerns that seem to be mirrored in the practice of adoption. However, not everyone working in the field of assisted reproductive technology accepts the notion that what has been learned in adoption is directly relevant to the practice of assisted reproduction. A stark example of this is found in England's House of Commons debates on the Human Fertilisation and Embryology Bill of 1990. The Secretary of State for Health rose in the House and declared: "...the relationship between someone who has been adopted and the natural parents who had to request that the child be adopted is different from the relationship, which in emotional terms is nonexistent, between a child and a donor of sperm" (Clarke, 1990). A parallel statement, describing the independence of adoption and embryo donations, may be found in the report, "Defining Embryo Donation" produced by the Ethics Committee of the American Society for Reproductive Medicine (2009): "...Application of the term 'adoption' to embryos is inaccurate, misleading, and could place burdens that are not appropriate for embryos that have been donated upon infertile recipients...adoption can not and does not apply to embryos, which hold the potential for life but are not persons...the procedures would place unwarranted burdens on the recipient patient(s)...who already face burdensome medical procedures in the pursuit of their fertility goals (p.1818-1819)." Note that there is no recognition of any potential psychological consequence for coming into the world through the use of assisted reproductive techniques and the use of donated genetic material from sources outside the family. Embryo donation is presented simply as tissue exchange, a material transaction between donor and recipient. Thus, from the perspectives of both governmental officials and medical practitioners of assisted reproduction, there is no link between the experiences of adoptees, adoptive parents and birth family on the one hand, and families created through reproductive technologies. The knowledge base of adoption is said not to illuminate an understanding of the experience of the offspring of assisted reproduction, and their social and genetic parents. However, before accepting such a conclusion, a deeper examination of these issues is clearly warranted.

Openness as a guiding principle of adoption practice is at the heart of our current thinking in the field. Today, parents choose to share their identities with families whom they have personally selected for the raising of their children. In most of the western world, outside of the United States, adult adoptees have rights to access birth parent identifying information. Even in the United States, there are five states that grant access to records and several others have legislation pending to open records. Moreover, open practice is not just the simple exchange of information. Today, it is becoming increasingly normative for birth and adoptive families to directly interact with each other over time. Sibling reconnection is seen as serving the needs of adopted children. Birth parents are no longer portrayed as a danger to the physical and psychological security of the adoptee. In fact, openness is seen to support the wellbeing of all those who are part of the adoption constellation (Grotevant & McRoy, 1998). Thus, if openness in adoption is thought to be foundational for establishing successful relationships between genetically unrelated individuals, then why has it been rejected as a basis for forming relationships in families created through assisted reproductive technology?

Blyth, Crawshaw, Hasse and Speirs (2001) have identified eight arguments offered by the professional practitioners of assisted reproductive technologies for operating in a closed system. While Blyth et al., (2001) direct their attention to the case of sperm donor insemination, for the purpose of this discussion, their points will be expanded to include two other situations, the donation of eggs and embryos.

The first argument mentioned by Blyth et al., is that secrecy will protect men from the stigma of infertility and presumed impotence. This is probably a reasonable assumption as fertility status is part of what it means to be "a man" at this point in our cultural history. Failure to live up to this genetic imperative is viewed as a weakness in the eyes of society. Offspring are a marker of masculinity and are living proof of the virility of the man. It is, therefore, not surprising that most men will go to some lengths to protect their narrative identities as "real" men.

The donation of an egg also reflects on the public fertility status of a woman. So much of our cultural understanding of family is bound up in the interplay of the nature and nurture of maternal roles. If the mother is not the one providing genetic material, then her status as mother is diminished by not living up to the full genetic ideal of giving birth to one's own genetic stock.

The third scenario involves using a donor embryo. This embryo may either be one left over from fertility treatments undertaken by other couples or may be specifically formed through the procuring of sperm and eggs from unrelated donors. Such a fertility strategy yields status challenges for both members of the couple as described for either sperm or egg donation. However, regardless of which of these three fertility strategies is used, the problem is that protecting one's fertility identity is done at the expense of the offspring's genetic identity, an issue all too common in the practice of adoption. This point is tied into the second reason that has been offered for using secrecy to hide the child's genetic history.

It is assumed that disclosing the fact that the child and parent or parents of the child do not share genetic material will negatively impact on the quality of the parent child relationship. Borrowing from the language of adoption and a consanguineous definition of family, the parent or parents who do not contribute to the child's genetic makeup are assumed to be fictive parents, that is, not "real" parents. From an evolutionary perspective, (Daly & Wilson, 1998), one serves in a parenting role for the explicit purpose of securing one's genetic expression into the next generation. If, however, the parent is not genetically related to the child, then one must, according to this view, create a fiction that will further the chances that the parents will treat the children as if they were genetic kin. Thus, secrecy is needed to maintain the myth of the child "as if having been born to the parents," a phrase common in adoption legislation up until the end of the twentieth century.

Some parents have chosen not to use gamete donation, even though one of the members of the couple is fertile, in an attempt to insure that there be balance in the relationship. Each parent starts a relationship with the child on an equal footing in that neither parent is more genetically privileged than the other. Again, no one asks what it will mean for the child to grow up with no genetic link to either parent. This silence is particularly distressing, given the fact that research in adoption has demonstrated that the search for genetic origins has become normative (Schechter and Bertocci, 1990).

The next reason offered for maintaining secrecy is that it will protect the family from the possible future intrusion of genetic donors into their lives. This concern has resonated in the adoption community where the secrecy of years past was offered as a means of keeping birth parents from returning and attempting to reclaim the child. The fact that this was a legal impossibility, as long as the adoption was facilitated under the rule of law, seemed to be of no consequence. Adoptive parents struggled to gain the status of parent. When children came under their legal wing, they remained ever vigilant to protect their sense of entitlement to parent.

With the advent of open practices in adoption, many initially expected that the fear of loosing a child to a birth parent would have increased. However, this has not proven to be so. With greater openness, there is a commensurate reduction in the fear adoptive parents have of loosing the child to a birth parent (Grotevant & McRoy, 1998). One would hope that this understanding of openness would have extended into the realm of families formed through assisted reproductive technology. However, this is not the case, either legally or psychologically. For assisted reproduction families, the law serves much less of a protective force than it does in adoption. In many jurisdictions, the legal status of parental responsibility and control falls under the law of material possession even though we are talking about family relationships. Genetic donation is seen as an exchange of property and not persons. Therefore, it is subject to considerations that leave feelings, commitment and relationships at the courtroom door. Today, in North America, there is no legislation governing adoption of embryos. Furthermore, when there are competing claims by the genetic donors, surrogate parents and receiving, social parents, there are no principles of adjudication for determining parental status other than the distribution of property. In such circumstances, is it little wonder that the positive relationship between openness and entitlement in adoption has had little influence over the intrusion fears of parents in assisted reproduction families. Clearly, if the inner rings of the constellation of assisted reproductive families are not to be distorted in the service of secrecy and protection of the integrity of the family, legislative protections must be more clearly established that leave no ambiguities surrounding parental rights. This must not be implemented, though, at the expense of the child's right to be able to construct a full and narratively truthful account of origins. We do not need to pit one competing interest against another. Both need to be respected.

The fourth reason that has been offered for secrecy is to protect the allegedly dubious moral reputations of the donors. Of course, the validity of such a proposition depends on the particular moral perspective one takes. There are those who believe that the obtaining of sperm for donation through masturbation is an immoral act as it is biblically proscribed. Others question the trafficking of eggs and sperm for financial gain or the renting of a womb by women who serve as surrogates. These acts are seen to cheapen life by treating embryonic development as an exchange of material objects and not potential sources of life. Finally, the moral integrity of couples who donate unused embryos has been cast in the same light as birth parents who have made a voluntary decision to place a child for adoption. In either case, the stigma of abandonment of kin, either born or yet to be born, is seen as breaching a natural imperative that parents are responsible for the raising of their children.

Clearly, the moral evaluation of all of these cases depends upon acceptance of wider spheres of thought about what is considered to be ethical behavior. If one views masturbation as devoid of meaning other than physical enjoyment of the act, then there is no stigma. If one donates gametes without payment, then the charge of commercialization of life is sidestepped. As for donations of embryos for placement with another family, either with or without adoption by the receiving couple, the moral judgment depends on two issues. The first is whether one accepts that destroying unused embryos created for fertility treatment is taking the life of a potential child or is simply the destruction of material that has no ability to sustain itself beyond the restricted conditions of the laboratory or womb. Principles of ethical adoption practice are silent on this issue. The other ethical challenge to embryo donation centers on the placement of a potential human being with individuals who may be ill prepared to meet the challenges of raising a child with whom they share no genetic connection. We have reached a point in the practice of adoption where screening of potential parents and pre placement education are required elements of facilitation, yet no major objection is raised with regards to those who are willing to accepted a donated embryo but have not been vetted for the psychological and material resources to raise a child. Furthermore, few cautionary concerns are offered in terms of what it will mean for a person to come into being as a result of assisted reproductive technology and then to live in the world without access to information or contact with part or all of one's genetic kin. A few lonely voices (Blyth et al., 2001; Cordary, 1997, 1999; Daniels, 1998; Daniels & Taylor, 1993) have argued that this issue reaches to the heart of the experience of offspring of assisted reproductive technology. However, those shaping policy and practice guidelines have cavalierly waved them off by stating that adoption and assisted reproduction share only minimal similarity. Regardless of the degree of similarity, experience and research in adoption currently serve as the only viable metaphor for what it is like to be raised by those who are not one's genetic kin. Until demonstrated otherwise, we must be vigilant to the needs of offspring of assisted reproduction in terms of access to information about origins, and the challenges of family dynamics without genetic similarity.

The next reason for maintaining secrecy is said to be to safeguard the donors of genetic material from any subsequent responsibility for the ensuing child. Typically, this is cast in terms of financial responsibility. To date, this has proven to be an unnecessary precaution as no court has yet to find donors to be required to meet the offspring's financials needs. These fall to the social parents as would be the case in adoption.

Are there other responsibilities that are not being articulated but should be? Again, accepting experience in adoption as a guide to practice, donors may not bare a financial responsibility but they do bare a psychological one to give their genetic offspring full information to construct a personal genetic narrative. Offspring need to know the history of their genetic kin, their special skills and aptitudes, their medical history and the reasons why donations of genetic material were made. Many offspring are motivated to become acquainted with genetic siblings, particularly, full genetic sisters and brothers. The desire to find those who share common traits, characteristics and appearance is very strong, indeed.

These arguments will sound familiar to adult adoptees. We are finally at the point where curiosity about origins is viewed as normal and not as a sign of pathology or a failed adoption. Such thinking must be extended into the realm of assisted reproduction. A narrative without the first chapter of one's existence leaves a person without a sense of personal gestalt (Sobol & Cardiff, 1983). Offspring of assisted reproduction did not ask to be put into the position of possessing a deficient narrative. They should have the same right as adoptees to know their origins. To countenance the use of assisted reproductive procedures without allowing access to one's history is the central issue of concern. Because gamete donation has these consequences, donors must either accept the responsibility of making identifying information available or decline to participate in such procedures. They, like birth parents do not necessarily have to enter into a relationship with their offspring, but they do owe them a history.

Another assumption in the field is that secrecy is necessary in order to encourage donors to come forward and participate in these procedures. In those jurisdictions where donation rates have dropped, lack of secrecy has been attributed as the cause. However, there may be other factors at work, particularly the fact that jurisdictions that have broken with secrecy also have made it illegal to receive payment for donation of genetic material. Therefore, it is difficult to tell which factor accounts for the decline in donation rates.

Again, reverting to the adoption literature, openness has not been an impediment to the decision to place a child for adoption. In fact, in those jurisdictions where there has been an opening of adoption records, there has also been an increase in rates of voluntary placements of infants (Sobol & Daly, 1994). In adoption today, genetic kin want to know the consequences of their decisions. We are just in the infancy of developing protocols in assisted reproductive practices. Surely, as thinking develops about appropriate courses of action, we should not be using a 1950 model of closed adoption as our guide. There have been no documented, negative repercussions for open adoption and ample evidence to indicate that openness is beneficial to all within the inner rings of the adoption constellation (Carp, 2007). There is nothing in the assisted reproduction literature to suggest that the case would not be the same.

Secrecy is also said to be necessary to ensure that the offspring will not be marked by the stigma of their origins as they, like adoptees, did not come into families as fully constituted, consanguineous members. Such a notion has little foundation. Families and their members come in so many varieties today that it is now quite impossible to put forward the two parent, heterosexual, consanguineous family as the normative standard. More than half of the children in North America do not live with both their genetic parents. Divorced, blended, step, single parent, and gay and lesbian families were all once stigmatized for being outside of the norm. Today, all are part of the cultural mosaic of family forms. There is no reason to assume that assisted reproduction families and their individual members are now so unique that they merit the assignment of a stigmatized status.

Another question arises around the issue of whether possessing knowledge of a different genetic history than one's parent or parents will affect the quality of relationships between parents and children? The question is an important one and one that requires much more research investigation. To date, most of the research has focused on donor insemination families, where the mother is genetically related to the child but the father is not. In these studies, few differences of a negative nature have been noted for parent-child relationships (Golombok, MacCallum, Goodman, & Rutter, 2002). What does emerge is a picture of relatively successful families. Mothers emotionally express warmth toward their children, while fathers take a less involved role in serious disputes with their children. It might be that mothers feel more entitlement to their parenting role as they are the genetic kin of the child and that fathers support them in that role. Golombok et al. (2002) also found that few children had been told of their genetic origins, yet this did not seem to impinge on their relationships. While such a conclusion may be justified by the data, it is important to consider the outcome of secrecy later in development. Judging by the experience of adoption, late revelation of the facts is typically accompanied by feeling of betrayal and a lack of subsequent trust. It is one thing to say that relationships at age 12 are within normal bounds when one does not know of one's genetic status. It is quite another thing to keep these relationships on an even keel following a late revelation. As Golombok et al. (2002) found that many people other than the child knew the genetic history of the child, it is clear that not telling of origins in the early life of the family sets up an explosive situation in the future if the secret is reveal. Secrecy does not secure the well being of relationships in the family. It puts them in jeopardy. Furthermore, even when parents have told their children the facts of their origin, the freedom to explore the meaning of this continued to be related to the quality of family relations. Like in adoption, open and respectful communications about origins took place in families with strong, positive relationships between parents and children (Berger & Paul, 2008).

Adoption has one final lesson for those who utilize assisted reproduction to form a family. At adulthood, particularly at meaningful developmental transitions, there will be a strong desire to know one's genetic ancestry and those who have been the source of one's DNA. Today, there are some jurisdictions in the western world that provide a means of gaining such information. Sweden, Austria and the United Kingdom, as well as a number of Australian states, the Netherlands, Norway, Finland, Switzerland and New Zealand have banned donor anonymity. Japan and Croatia are considering doing so. In Germany, where egg donation is banned, it has been established that offspring have the right to identify a biological parent, although no case has yet been tried in the courts. Sadly, missing from this list are Canada and the United States, the most active users of assisted reproduction.

I believe that it is unethical to bring a life into existence through the use of assisted reproductive means and then deny the resulting person the same rights as all other citizens (other than adoptees in too many jurisdictions) to an accurate and honest genetic history.

We need government administered registries that will track identifying information and hold it either until the resulting embryo
is an adult or the case arises that there is a medical emergency that
merits knowing a complete genetic, medical history. If donors are
not willing to participate in full disclosure of identifying information at the offspring's age of adulthood, then they should be banned
from donating genetic material. Additionally, if they are interested
in developing a relationship with their genetic children, then a
registry should help to facilitate this possibility. It is time to stop
treating assisted reproduction only as a technological challenge.
It also has a profound effect upon narrative identity. Surely, truth
and openness must serve as its foundational principles.

CHAPTER 6

TAKING OUR PRINCIPLES
TO THE STREETS

Turn from evil and do good, Seek peace and pursue it. (Psalm 34)

At the heart of an understanding of the adoption constellation as a theoretical metaphor is the notion that as a systemic model, all levels of the constellation interact. The advantage of such a model over the concepts of adoption triad or adoptive kinship network (Grotevant, Ross, Marchel, & McRoy, 1999) is that spheres of influence beyond the adoptive and birth family are always part of our understanding of adoption and hence, are not pushed off to a corner where they are dealt with as totally separate phenomena. When we think of adoptive family life, we quickly recognize that extended birth and adoptive family, and community members both close (teachers, physicians, social workers, friends and acquaintances) and far (members of the media, policy makers and legislators) all play contributing roles in the life-long process of adoption. In the day-to-day experience of those at the center of the constellation, proximal interactions are of most importance. However, when focusing upon the wider themes that are developed within an adoptive family, such as openness, narrative identity and honesty, we are now able to see how community attitudes about what constitutes appropriate behavior is reflected in social legislation, the outer ring of the adoption constellation.

Adoption legislation dictates what constitutes a family. The law determines the legal status of family members, the degree to which historical truth will be altered in the service of moving an adoptive family from fictive to legitimate status, who may give consent to the adoption and whether the family of origin will be granted any role in the on-going life of the adoptive family.

Different members of the constellation experience the gravitational pull of legislation at distinct points in the developmental process of adoption. How the law delineates the boundaries of an uncontested facilitation of an adoption will determine the degree to which the parent whose child is being placed will make volitional choices as to the placement and beyond. The law will describe who may play professional roles in this event. It will place limits on what information may be exchanged and who will have access to such information in the future. The name of the child will be changed and typically, documentary evidence of a history prior to placement will be sealed. Parental rights and authority will be transferred to the adoptive parents, so they will be treated as the only parents of the child. However, in most cases, the law will block them from gaining access to the child's birth kin, even when the adoptive parents believe it is in the child's best interests to do so. In jurisdictions with sealed records, adult adoptees will have no rights to identifying information. This is said to serve the myth that adoptees share genetic history with their adoptive parents. Furthermore, the law will often treat birth parents as being in need of protection from any future exposure of the alleged sins of their youth. When considering all of these restrictions on personal choice, it is truly paradoxical that those members of society who are most concerned with keeping the state out of the lives of its citizens often are those who most fully embrace legal restrictions on birth and adoptive families managing their own relationships.

Fortunately, in spite of the restrictions that still appear in many jurisdictions, we are beginning to see a new era in adoption legislation. In several countries, the law recognizes the importance of open relationships and seeks to preserve them. In most European countries, New Zealand, six states of the United States, and several Australian states and Canadian provinces, adult adoptees are granted the right to a full history and the names of their birth parents. In the Canadian context, birth parents may also obtain the adoptive names of their children when the children reach adulthood. Some laws grant this information without restriction. Others provide the opportunity to place an information veto on the record. In Britain, there are no restrictions on access to information for adult adoptees. In Canada, for all adoptions finalized after the passing of the legislation, adult adoptees and birth parents will be granted access to identifying information without restriction.

One of the arguments that often has been advanced for keeping records closed is that birth parents were promised future confidentiality. There are several problems with this position. The first is that an examination of the legal documents signed at the time of placement and finalization will reveal that the law was silent on the issue of future confidentiality. These documents refer only to the loss of parental rights, not management of an identity. This being the case, adherents of closed records claim that birth parents may not have signed documents granting confidentiality but they went into the adoption with the understanding that they would have such confidentiality forever. However, those lawyers and social workers who made such statements had no legal authority to do so as the legislation was silent about the possibility of opening in the future. Finally, as many birth mothers have publically stated at legislative hearings considering new legal proposals, they were not promised confidentiality but access to identifying information when their children became legal adults. Of course, this promise also has proven to be without foundation in too many jurisdictions.

As the door on legislative reform is beginning to crack open, many groups are rallying across the western world to find legislative solutions to sealed records. Too often, their labors come to naught as they flail away against the legislative bulwarks, expending great effort but generating little success. The result is a demoralized adoption community, once again experiencing many of the core issues of an adoptive narrative identity, particularly a sense of helpless, and a belief that their pain will never end. As such, not having an authentic first chapter of their lives is a sign that they matter little to those who write and administer legislation. Fortunately, not all efforts have met with failure. Some jurisdictions have responded positively to the message of the activist community to open records. Ontario is one of the most recent to do so. Several important lessons were learned in this campaign and they shall be discussed in turn[19].

On June 1, 2009, all adoptees became eligible to receive their original sealed birth registration forms. Their birth parents were entitled to receive the adoption order with their child's adoptive name, but the name of the adoptive parents removed. Regrettably, an information veto was granted to either party blocking release of such information if the other party so wished. A contact preference form was also included in the legislation with penalties for its violation. Finally, the new law stated that for all new adoptions, when the child became a legal adult, adoptee and birth parents would have unrestricted access to identifying information about the other. Records would finally be fully opened.

To achieve this piece of legislation, many hurdles needed to be crossed. The struggle spanned four decades in all. However, with the passing of years, small changes were implemented that led to the push to bring about the current legislation. Fortuitously, a group of activists, sat together on the board of the Adoption Council of

---

19   The following ideas reflect a continuing dialogue that I have had with my two colleagues, Karen Lynn, president of the Canadian Council of Natural Mothers and Wendy Rowney, president of Adoption Search and Kinship. Together, the three of us make up the coordinating committee of the Coalition for Open Adoption Records, Ontario. I would also like to acknowledge the contributions of COAR's predecessor, the Adoption Reform Coalition of Ontario and two of its key members, Monica Byrne, President of Parent Finders Canada, and Pat McCarron, president of Parent Finders, National Capital Region. Jim Kelly, Joan Vanstone and Nancy Kato, leaders of the campaign to open records in British Columbia have also been important influences in my thinking. I shall remain ever grateful for all of the wisdom that each one of them has shared with me over the years of struggle to open records in Canada.

Ontario in the early part of the first decade of this century. They recognized that in order to bring about change, there needed to be a focused effort, one that would gather the collective voices within the adoption community and would, in unity, speak forcefully to members of the Provincial Legislature. Thus, the Coalition for Open Adoption Records (COAR) came into being. Our struggle taught us many lessons about community organization and advocacy. These are presented in the hope that they will assist those who will take up the torch to bring an end to a closed system of adoption.

Advocacy Strategies

Be Patient, Committed and Persistent

There is no better lesson to learn. The legislative process is not a simple or straightforward one. It will take time to learn the mechanics of how it operates, where pressure might be applied, how to use the press, where friends and supporters might be found. Even more important than these simple nuts and bolts of political action, one must learn to cope with long delays in gratification for effort expended. There has rarely been a political push for change that has taken less than a decade. If you are only able to sustain motivation in situations where there is immediate reinforcement for effort, the political domain is not for you. Also, to be a successful adoption reform advocate, one must find the resources to deal with setbacks. As the political stripes of governments changed following elections or bureaucrats were periodically replaced, it was necessary to begin the process of educating and advocating anew, often starting at step one. We had the experience of witnessing the most progressive piece of open record legislation in the world (with no restrictions on access to identifying information for adult adoptees and birth parents) struck down by the courts, just two days after it had come into effect. The very next day, we were making contacts with our allies in the Government, writing letters to the editor and rallying our community of supporters. It felt like we were Sisyphus of Greek mythology, condemned to carry a heavy rock up a steep hill, only to have it roll to the bottom every time he approached the summit. Our advocacy was analogous, except that we were committed to persist until we saw a better law on the books. It can be a long journey, but not one without end for those who are stout hearted.

Establish a Strong Leadership Core

In an ideal world, the adoption community would come together with a common goal and a unified voice. Of course, such a possibility is rarely, if ever, achieved. Typically, community members strike out in different directions. The effect of their collective efforts is diluted in that no clear position is articulated that legislators will perceive to be representative of the community's desire for change. This becomes important as politicians are less interested in an idea than whether the idea has support within a constituency of voters. Thus, to achieve a focused message, it becomes necessary to concentrate decision-making and communications within a representative group that reflects the views of the community.

To this end, we organized a small coordinating committee drawn from the major adoption advocacy groups across the province. We sought out individuals with a track record of community leadership, who possessed the kinds of social skills that allowed for effective participation within the coordinating committee and engagement with the wider community and legislators. In particular, people were selected who had the authority to speak on behalf of large constituencies.

One also has to consider how large the group should be to operate in a maximally effective manner. Our experience was the smaller the group, the better. There is less opportunity for conflict, fewer cliques are likely to emerge and intergroup communication is more straightforward. That being said, the group must not be so small that parts of the community feel they have been disenfranchised by not having a member on the coordinating committee. Thus, a balance must be struck that both makes the workings of the group efficient, and permits community members to feel that their voices are being heard. In the end, COAR had a coordinating committee of three. However, recognizing that we needed more community input, we made a concentrated effort to bring many others into the process for consultation, advice and to externally represent our collective efforts. Failure to utilize others in a leadership capacity would have isolated us from the community. We would have been seen as not advocating fully on behalf of the community but rather as serving our own needs. Judging by the feedback we received, I think we succeeded in finding an effective balance.

Choose a Name for Your Coalition

It is necessary to give your group a meaningful name that will spearhead your efforts to bring about new legislation. It is recommended that an acronym be chosen that not only is short, solid, and trustworthy but which also captures the essence of what you hope to accomplish. We settled on the Coalition to Open Adoption Records (Ontario), or COAR. Although the spelling is different, the fact this acronym sounded the same as the word "core" allowed us to remind everyone (the community, the press and legislators, alike) that we were pressing for the core issue in the life of adult adoptees and birth parents, that of access to open records. This label caught on immediately and served as a quick and effective mnemonic for remembering who we were and what we stood for.

Establish an Air of Professionalism

Whenever the public encounters your group, regardless of the medium of the message, there must be an air of professionalism that pervades your communication. This is accomplished in many different ways. Letterhead and business cards must be consistent in format and convey essential information such as the name of the group, the name of the person and his or her specific portfolio, email address, postal address and contact phone numbers. If room permits, a mission phrase that captures the essence of the legislative initiative should also be included. Never use a written document before it has been checked for grammar and spelling. Such mistakes take away from the credibility of your message. Thus, there should be a commitment to be scrupulous in ensuring that every document is presented in a professional manner.

Create an Internet Presence

This is a good place to seek assistance from the community. There are always individuals who are willing to serve as webmasters. The site should be easy to navigate. Visitors to the site must be able to quickly locate information about the goals of the legislative initiative, the current status of the legislation, how they can contact the coordinating committee and most importantly, what they can personally do to further the cause. The internet is an indispensible medium for keeping the community informed and motivated to turn their passion for the issue of adoption reform into constructive action. For example, we used the site to encourage others to make copies of our petition and to collect signatures to support the cause. This allowed us to demonstrate to the legislature that support for an open records bill came from one end of Ontario to the other.

Over the course of the campaign to open records, thousands of individuals contacted us voicing support and suggestions. To further their involvement and to ensure that we did not stray from the position of the community, we created an email group on Yahoo, using COAR as its name. Updates were disseminated to the community on a regular basis, informing them of where the bill currently stood, and what had been done in the period since the last message to the group. This forum also served as a means of encouraging the community to let us know their thoughts on the campaign, and as a motivational tool for getting individuals to participate in specific undertakings.

At a critical point in the campaign, it became necessary to mount a legal defense of an open records bill. Using our contact list, we asked the community to decide whether we should undertake this costly venture. Their votes came in the form of donations to a legal defense fund. Within a brief period of time, we were able to garner enough funds to cover our legal costs. Without such a speedy means of presenting this province-wide request, it would have been impossible to have legal representation. Although costly, the generosity of the community proved to be a strong indication of their commitment to put a personal mark on the outcome of the campaign.

Learn the Rules for the Creation and Distribution of Press Releases

One of the keys to a successful reform campaign is to learn to use the media to publicize your position on needed changes in legislation. The first line of attack is to learn to produce effective press releases. The media receive hundreds of these a day. Therefore, if yours does not stand out in some way, it will be quickly lost in the shuffle. Make sure that you follow the local template used to identify press releases for each region has different requirements for what must be included. Again, it is important to check all documents for spelling and grammar. Keep your message brief and to the point but try to include one distinguishing twist on the current discussion of the issues. This will encourage the media to pursue your story. Finally, include contact information for those individuals you want the media to interview.

Use Skilled Spokespersons

Spokespersons for the group must always be articulate, knowledgeable and respectful. Not only are they the face of the organization, but also individuals whose lives serve as exemplars of the need for legislative reform. It is important to choose a style of dress that also reflects the professionalism of the spokespersons. I am not suggesting that fashion will be a determining factor in bringing about change. However, a spokesperson should never do anything that takes one off message. Causal attire, in the formal setting of legislative hearings, diminishes the authority of the message when those who should be concentrating on our words instead focus on our style of dress.

It is of primary importance that spokespersons can think on their feet. Often, we found ourselves being confronted by persistent reporters who tried to put words in our mouths in order to generate a much more controversial story for themselves. Spokespersons must not become easily flustered by microphones, television cameras and impertinent questions. They must approach every encounter, having reviewed possible issues that might arise, and having practiced possible answers that best convey the messages that they want to be heard. To implement this, it is necessary to have a strong knowledge base of all adoption matters. This is rarely something that one individual can accomplish. Therefore, we tried to insure that the coordinating committee of COAR was always present at press gatherings. One of us was a birth mother who knew the key issues of the birth parent experience, particularly the details of past facilitation practices, the nature of the legal documents that had been signed and the communications between social worker and parent. A second spokesperson was an adoptee and a trained historian. She had a commanding knowledge of the laws of adoption, both domestic and foreign, and could cite chapter and verse when others were misrepresenting the law. Finally, as an adoptee and a psychologist with an extensive background in adoption research and clinical work, I was able to speak with authority about the knowledge base in the field. I also believe that my titles, "Dr" and "Professor" gave my words substantial gravitas. I offer this last point not to diminish the skills of my colleagues but to reflect on the fact that, often times, audiences are swayed by the least important characteristics of one's message.

Always be Prompted in Requests for Information

Today, the primary medium of communication is the internet. Email has a tendency to flood any organization's capacity to respond. Nevertheless, a quick turn around of messages tells the community that you are interested in their ideas and you wish them to be part of the movement. It also sends the message to legislators and bureaucrats that you are a professional team that is made up of responsive and competent individuals.

One of the issues that discourages efficacious communication is the need to repeat a message over and over as new requests for information are received. To this end, it is suggested that a series of prepared responses be created but that discretion be used when using them as each person must feel that he or she is receiving your full attention.

Finally, we retained the email address of every person who wrote to us. If they shared our views or offered support, they were placed on our email distribution list. Quickly, we gathered hundreds of supporters who could be counted on to spread our message well beyond the confines of the group. This exponential growth in supporters is one of the key markers of a successful campaign.

The strategies that have been offered up to this point deal with structural matters. I will now turn attention to strategies that are more process oriented.

Build a Coalition of Supporting Groups and Organizations

Coalitions are typically built to insure that a particular message is clearly heard by those who will make decisions about what goes into legislation. If a cacophony of voices is heard, then the conclusion drawn is that the community is split and there is no consensus on what should go into the legislation. Therefore, every effort must be directed toward bringing together as wide and as influential a grouping of those who will support your position. This can be accomplished in two ways.

The first strategy is to convene a gathering of key players and hammer out a common position that will be supported by each player's constituency. This is a challenging task as it may be quite difficult to establish a consensus. Nevertheless, COAR took the chance by gathering together the province's largest adoptive parent group, the provincial umbrella organization of agencies offering child welfare and placement services, adoption search and reunion groups and the Canadian Council of Natural Mothers, the largest birth mother collective in the country. Those representing each party were not natural allies, nor had they had particularly good relations in the past. However, we were determined to sit down together and not leave until a consensus had been reached. Fortunately, there were a few at the table who sat in more than one camp and they served as facilitators for our deliberations. Possessing cross-group credibility enhanced their ability to broker a deal. It was not easy. All of us compromised to some extent, but in the end, we walked out of these deliberations with a shared vision of what direction the new law must take. Some might see this as having made a deal with the devil. After all, many of these groups had spoken out against open records in the past. However, we were determined to keep our eye on the goal. If those who had opposed us now came on side, we said thank you. The cause of open records was simply too important to let old wounds get in the way of changing the law.

The second strategy that we used to build a coalition was to seek out endorsements from groups across the province. Each organization publically endorsed the position we held, and accepted COAR as the group who would speak with governmental officials and the media. This was a tremendous advantage when we met with key legislative players. The granting of wide approval as the community's voice, gave us much more power in our deliberations. Legislators were more willing to support our position, knowing that there was major support for legislative change from adoptees, birth parents, adoptive parents, social workers, mental health professionals offering adoption services, and thousands of citizens who had signed our petitions. Therefore, whenever we introduced ourselves, we never failed to list all the groups who endorsed our position. It not only gave us credibility for being able to gather such support, but it also gave our objectives the stamp of approval of all the major groups concerned with various aspects of adoption.

One final point should be made. Although endorsements from large adoption groups were critical to our success, selected endorsements from individuals were also important as well. For example, as discussions with legislators progressed, it became clear that while some appreciated the psychological damage brought about by closed records, most were interested in the need for adoptees to obtain a complete medical history. In order to translate this interest into motivation to change the law, we needed an authoritative medical voice to educate legislators about the health risks of not having access to such information for birth families, adoptees and their own children. Thus, we sought out a distinguished medical geneticist to add his voice to the cause. We then introduced him to legislators at a reception held in support of the bill. He minced no words in stating that people were dying because they did not have a full medical history of their genetic kin. This was a powerful message and one we carried personally into all subsequent deliberations.

Find a Legislative Champion

There are few in the adoption community who possess finely attuned political skills. Most of us may know a great deal about the experience of adoption, however, changing legislation is a very different matter, indeed. It is necessary, therefore, to find champions who are able to maneuver through the political landscape. Typically, this person is a legislator with a direct connection to adoption. In our case, a senior member of one of the minority parties, a birth mother who had a long-standing relationship with her son, came to our assistance. She provided us with astute advice about the steps leading to the passage of a bill. She also assisted us in gaining access to individuals who might not have met with us without a gentle phone call on her part. We were also fortunate to have contact with legislative assistants who helped to steer us in the right direction as we shaped our messages and sought out opportunities of influence. Such advice was invaluable and much appreciated.

Develop a Thick Skin

It is a sad reality that the strongest personal criticism we received did not come from legislators, social workers or adoptive parents. Instead, it came from a small group of adoptees. This did not surprise me. Adoption can be a very painful experience for some, and when emotions cut deeply, one strikes out at those who are closest to you. Fortunately, this did not occur very often but when it did, we needed to be mindful of what was happening. First, we had to ask why they were objecting to our position. Were we being obtuse in our communications? Had we failed to hear their concerns? Had we isolated ourselves from the community? Were we perceived as elitists, taking power into our own hands? All of these are legitimate concerns and might have served as the basis for the anger we received. It is also possible to think of the anger, to paraphrase Erving Goffman, as normal behavior in a crazy situation. Frustration for being denied the right to a veridical history quite naturally leads to verbal aggression. From here, it is but a small step to displacing such anger onto those nearest to you. And why should adult adoptees not be angry? For too long, they and their birth parents have waited, demanded and been denied legitimacy. However, if one is a political activist, then an outward public expression of anger is not on the agenda, no matter what its source. Anger demonstrates weakness and psychological insecurity. Politicians are always looking for reasons not to open records. We definitely do not need to give them one. Remaining calm in the face of personal attack, most importantly, keeps one focused on the goal. To turn aside and counter attack does nothing to gain open records. Being mindful of one's purpose allows energy to be focused constructively. This is not easy to do. Striking out may bring immediate satisfaction. However, it has no ultimate value. To be a successful advocate for open records, a thick skin impervious to personal assault must be our amour, a just cause our might and clarity of focus, our goal.

Do Not Forget Your Own Family

In the struggle to open records, all of us found it difficult to remember that others, close to us, were impacted by our actions and focus. Long hours of meetings, travel to other parts of the province and the time needed to keep up with the moment-to-moment demands, took us away from our families. They were the ones to pick up the slack caused by our focus on the campaign. It is, therefore, very important to acknowledge and thank them for their behind the scenes support which gave us the freedom to meet the challenge of changing the law.

Never Give Up

When COAR was formed, we committed ourselves to the task of opening adoption records. We were determined to persist with the task until adoptees and birth parents had the right to access the very same information as all other adult citizens of our province. What this commitment meant was that we had to learn to continually press forward, even when we saw our hard work dashed against the rocks of political and legal impediments. More than once, a bill received initial support, only to die on the books prior to final legislative approval. Our response to setbacks was to have a bill before the legislators at all times. They had to know that we could not be pushed aside. We would not disappear. We would not become resigned to crumbs. We would stand before them, month in and month out, year in and year out, until they passed a bill granting access to one's identity. This determination kept our issues alive. We were like a little terrier grabbing at a trouser leg. We would not let go. Petitions would continue to be presented. Waves of email would greet them, urging a change in the law. When we could not obtain a government bill, we found a means of placing a minority party bill before them. It had no chance of passage, but it kept them talking about open records.

In the end, we had a bill that passed. It did not give us every-thing we wanted but it moved our province many steps forward. Adult adoptees and birth parents became entitled to identifying information. For a short period of time, prior to the implementa-tion of the law, an information veto could be filed. Once the filing date had past, all adoptions prior to the bill that did not have an information veto would be opened. For those adoptions facilitated after the bill, records would be opened without restriction at the point when the adoptee became an adult. Finally, the bill gave adoptees and birth parents a means of managing their relationships through the use of a contact preference with penalties if it were to be violated. Would I have preferred a bill without any vetoes? Absolutely. There is **no** evidence that they are needed (Carp, 2007). We had to make a decision: either accept only perfection or take a practical stance and support a piece of legislation that dramatic-ally improves access to open records. We chose the latter. We felt it was the correct decision. Do not think, however, that our work is done. The day after the implementation of the bill, we were already talking about what was needed to achieve a better piece of legislation. Respectful treatment under the law may be our right but it will require unrelenting effort. Politicians have rarely let a well-gathered fact get in the way of a strongly held opinion. They are a stubborn lot, but so are we. We will achieve open records for all in adoption. It will happen because we will make it so.

A Final Thought

When I reflect back on adoption of the 1950's and 60's, it is clear we have come a long way. No responsible or knowledgeable person continues to advocate for secrecy and shame as foundational principles of adoption. The tide of open records is rising across the Western world. New forms of adoption and other alternatives for defining families are emerging. Birth parents, particularly mothers, no longer hide away with their pain and deep sadness. Adoptees are stepping forward to claim their full, authentic and truthful narrative identities. Adoptive parents appear who are exemplars of open and respectful persons in relationship with birth families. In professional social work, more are recognizing the impact of past practices: the damage that was done in the name of the best interests of the child when, in fact, the profession was actually serving the best interests of adoptive parents, the state, and themselves. We have much to atone for the mistakes of the past and yet to be fair, at the time it might not have seemed so. Extracting ourselves from the wider cultural context in which we live is a most difficult task. Few of us can claim skill at doing so.

And so, how will the ideas that have been championed in these pages be viewed by those who might be touched by them in generations to come? I can only hope that they will be received as an offering, given in the spirit of respect, compassion and the desire to build strong and caring relationships. If they fail to meet this mark, I ask for forgiveness. If they bring a lessening of pain and an increased sense of well being, it has been worth the effort.

REFERENCES

American Society for Reproductive Medicine Ethics Committee. (2009). Defining embryo donation. *Fertility and Sterility, 92 (6),* 1818-1819.

Bachrach, C. A., Adams, P. F., Sambrano, S., & London, K. A. (1989). Advanced data: Adoption in the 1980's (From Vital and Health Statistics No. 181). Hyattsville, MD: National Center for Health Statistics.

Berger, R., & Paul, M, (2008). Family secrets and family functioning: The case of donor assistance. *Family Process, 47,* 553–566.

Blyth, E., Crawshaw, M., Haase, J., &and Speirs, J. (2001). The implications of adoption for donor offspring following donor-assisted conception. *Child and Family Social Work, 6,* 295–304.

Bohman, M. (1970). Adopted children and their families: A follow-up study of adopted children, their background, environment and adjustment. Stockholm: Proprius.

Bohman, M., & Sigvardsson, S. (1990). Outcome in adoption: Lessons from longitudinal studies. In D. Brodzinsky & M. Schechter (eds.), *The psychology of adoption.* (pp. 93-106). New York: Oxford University Press.

Borders, L. D., & Penny, J. M., Portnoy, F. (2000). Adult Adoptees and Their Friends: Current Functioning and Psychosocial Well-Being. *Family Relations, 49 (4),* 407-418.

Bowlby, J. (1969). Attachment and loss. Vol. 1. Attachment. New York: Basic Books.

Bowlby, J. (1973). Attachment and loss. Vol. 2. Separation. New York: Basic Books.

Bowlby, J. (1980). Attachment and loss. Vol.3. Loss: Sadness, and depression. New York: Basic Books.

Brodzinsky, D. M. (1993). Long-term outcomes in adoption. The Future of Children, 93, 153-166.

Brodzinsky, D. M., Lang, R., & Smith, D. W. (1995). Parenting adopted children. In M. H. Bornstein, (Ed.), Handbook of parenting, Vol. 1, (pp.209-232). Mahwah, NJ: Lawrence Erlbaum.

Brodzinsky, D. M., Radice, C., Huffman, L., & Merkler, K. (1987). Prevalence of clinically significant symptomatology in a non-clinical sample of adopted and nonadopted children. *Journal of Clinical Child Psychology, 16,* 350-356.

Brodzinsky, D., & Steiger, C. (1991). Prevalence of adoptees among special education populations. *Journal of Learning Disabilities, 24,* 484-489.

Carp, E. W. (2007). Does opening adoption records have an adverse social impact? Some lessons from the US., Great Britain, and Australia, 1953-2007. *Adoption Quarterly, 10(3),* 29-52.

Cassidy, J., & Shaver, P. R. (1999). Handbook of attachment : theory, research, and clinical applications. New York : Guilford Press.

Cadoret, R. J. (1990). Biological perspectives on adoptee adjustment. In D. Brodzinsky & M. D. Schechter (Eds.), The psychology of adoption (pp.25-41). New York: Oxford University Press.

Cohen, N. J., Coyne, J., & Duvall, J. (1993). Adopted and biological children in the clinic: Family, parental and child characteristics. *Journal of Child Psychology and Psychiatry, 34,* 545-562.

Cordray, A.W. (1997) The need for a sense of self-identity. In: Donor Conception Support Group of Australia Inc. (Ed.), Let the offspring speak: Discussions on donor conception (pp. 35–38). New South Wales: Georges Hall.

Cordray, A.W. (1999/2000) A survey of people conceived through donor insemination. *DI Network News,* 14, 4–5.

Daly, K. (1988). Reshaped parental identity: The transition to adoptive parenthood. *Journal of Contemporary Ethnography, 17,* 40-66.

Daly, K and Sobol, M. P. (1993). Adoption in Canada: The National Adoption Study of Canada. University of Guelph: Guelph, Ontario.

Daly, K., & Sobol, M. P. (1994). Public and private adoption: A comparison of service and accessibility. *Family Relations, 43,* 86-93.

Daly, M., & Wilson, M. (1998). *The truth about Cinderella: A Darwinian view of parental love.* London, England: Orion Publishing Group.

Daniels, K. (1998). The sperm providers. In K. Daniels & E. Haimes (eds.), Donor insemination: International social science perspectives (pp. 76–104). Cambridge: Cambridge University Press.

Daniels, K. & Taylor, K. (1993). Secrecy and openness in donor insemination. *Politics and the Life Sciences, August,* 155–168.

Davis, C. (2002).. Women's accounts of resilience following child sexual abuse: A narrative study. *Dissertation Abstracts International: Section B: The Sciences & Engineering, Vol 61(12-B),* 2001. pp. 6700. [Dissertation Abstract

Dixon, L. A., Scheidegger, C., & McWhirter, J. J. (2009). The adolescent mattering experience:

Gender variations in perceived mattering, anxiety, and depression. *Journal of Counseling and Development, 87,* 302-310.

Doka, K. (1989). Disenfranchised grief : recognizing hidden sorrow. Lexington, Mass: Lexington Books.

Doka, K. J. (2002) Disenfranchised Grief: New Directions, Challenges and Strategies for Practices. Rescance Press, Champaign, IL.

Doka, K. J. (2008). Disenfranchised grief in historical and cultural perspective. In Stroebe, Margaret S.; Hansson, Robert O.; Schut, Henk; Stroebe, Wolfgang; Van den Blink, Emmy (2008). *Handbook of bereavement research and practice: Advances in theory and intervention.* (pp. 223-240). Washington, DC, US: American Psychological Association.

Frisk, M. (1964). Identity problem and confused conceptions of the genetic ego in adopted children during adolescence. *Acta Paedo Psychiatrica, 31,* 6-12.

Furstenberg, F. (1995). Fathering in the inner city: Paternal participation and public policy. In W. Marsiglio (Ed.), *Fatherhood:*

Contemporary theory, research, and social policy. (pp. 119-147). Thousand Oaks: Sage.

Gjerdingen, D. K., & Froberg, D. (1991). Predictors of health in new mothers. *Social Science & Medicine, 33(12)*, 1399-1407.

Goffman, E. (1963). *Stigma: Notes on the Management of Spoiled Identity.* New York, NY: Prentice-Hall.

Goldberg, D., & Wolkind, S. N. (1992). Patterns of psychiatric disorder in adopted girls: A research note. *Journal of Child Psychology and Psychiatry, 33*, 935-940.

Graafsma, T. L. G., Bosma, H. A., Grotevant, H. D., & deLevita, D. J. 1994). Identity and development: An interdisciplinary view. In Bosma, H. A., Graafsma, T. L. G., Grotevant, H. D., & deLevita, D. J. (1994). *Identity and development: An interdisciplinary approach.* (pp. 159-174). Thousand Oaks, CA: Sage.

Grand, M. P. (2006). Adoption through a retrospective lens: Implications for post adoption service. In M. M. Dore, (Ed.), *The post adoptive experience: Adoptive families' service needs and service outcomes.* (pp. 45-64). Washington, D.C.: Child Welfare League of America.

Grotevant, H. D. (1997). Coming to terms with adoption: The construction of identity from adolescence into adulthood. *Adoption Quarterly, 1*, 3-27.

Grotevant, H. D., Dunbar, N., Kohler, J. K., & Lash Esau, A. M. (2000). Adoptive identity: How contexts within and beyond the family shape developmental pathways. *Family Relations, 49*, 379-387.

Grotevant, H. D., & McRoy, R. (1998). Openness in adoption. Thousand Oaks, CA: Sage.

Grotevant, H. D., McRoy, R. G., & Jenkins, V. Y. (1988). Emotionally disturbed, adopted adolescents: Early patterns of family adaptation. *Family Process, 27*, 439-457.

Grotevant, H. D., Ross, N. M., Marchel, M. A., & McRoy, R. G. (1999). Adaptive behavior in adopted children: Predictors from early risk, collaboration in relationships within the adoptive kinship network, and openness arrangements. *Journal of Adolescent Research*, *14*, 231-247.

Guggenheim, M. (2005). What's Wrong with Children's Rights. Boston, MA.:Harvard University Press.

Haugaard, J. J. (1998). Is adoption a risk factor for the development of adjustment problems? *Clinical Psychology Review*, *18*, 47-69.

Hoopes, J. L. (1982). Prediction in child development: A longitudinal study of adoptive and nonadoptive families. New York: Child Welfare League of America.

Humphrey, M., & Kirkwood, R. (1982). Marital relationship among adopters. *Adoption and Fostering*, *6*, 44-48.

Jeffrey, C. R. (1962). Social class and adoption practices. *Social Problems*, *9*, 354-358.

Juffer, F,. & Rosenboom, L.G. (1997). Infant-mother attachment of internationally adopted children in the Netherlands. *International Journal of Behavioral Development*, *20*, 93-107.

Kagan, J (1994). Galen's prophecy : temperament in human nature. New York : Basic Books, 1994.

Kirk, D. (1964). Shared fate. New York: The Free Press.

Kotsopoulos, S., Cote, A., Joseph, L., Pentland, N., Stavrakki., C., Sheahan, P., & Oke, L. (1988). Psychiatric disorders in adopted children: A controlled study. *American Journal of Orthopsychiatry*, *58*, 608-611.

Lempert, L. B. (1999). Other fathers: An alternative perspective on African American community caring. In R. Staples (Ed.), The Black family: Essays and Studies (pp. 189-201). Belmont, CA: Wadsworth.

Lewis, M. (1997). Altering fate: Why the past does not predict the future. New York: Guilford Press.

Lifton, B. J. (1994). Journey of the adopted self: A quest for wholeness. New York: Basic Books.

Loehlin, L. C., Willerman, L., & Horn, J. M. (1982). Personality resemblances between unwed mothers and their adopted-away offspring. *Journal of Personality and Social Psychology, 42,* 1089-1099.

Leon, I. G. (2002). Adoption losses: Naturally occurring or socially constructed? *Child Development, 73,* 652-663.

Marshall, S. K. (2001). Do I matter? Construct validation of adolescents' perceived mattering to parents and friends. *Journal of Adolescence, 24,* 473–490.

McCarty, C., Waterman, J., & Burge, D. (1999). Experiences, concerns, and service needs of families adopting children with prenatal substance exposure: Summary and recommendations. *Child Welfare, 78 (5),* 561-577.

McGlone, K., Santos, L., & Kazama, L. (2002) Psychological stress in adoptive parents of special-needs children. *Child Welfare, 81(2),* 151-171.

Mech, E. V. (1973). Adoption: A policy perspective. In B. Caldwell & H. N. Ricciuti (Eds.), Review of child development research (Vol. 3, pp. 467-507). Chicago: University of Chicago Press.

Modell, J. (1994). Kinship with strangers: adoption and interpretations of kinship in American culture. Berkeley, London: University of California Press.

Oliver, P. J., & Srivastava, S. (1999). The Big-five trait taxonomy: History, measurement, and theoretical perspectives. In L. Pervin and O.P. John (Eds.), Handbook of personality: Theory and research (2nd ed.). New York: Guilford (1999).

Piersma, H. L. (1987). Adopted children and inpatient psychiatric treatment: A retrospective study. *The Psychiatric Hospital, 18,* 153-158.

Plomin, R., & DeFries, J. C. (1985). The origins of individual differences in infancy: The Colorado adoption project. New York: Academic Press.

Priel, B., Melamed-Hass, S., Besser, A., & Kantor, B. (2000). Adjustment among adopted children: The role of maternal self-reflectiveness. *Family Relations, 49,* 389-396.

Robinson, E. B. (2000). Adoption and loss: The hidden grief. Christies Beach, South Australia: Clova Publications.

Rogeness, G. A., Hoppe, S. K., Macedo, C .A., Fischer, C., & Harris, W. R. (1988). Psychopathology in hospitalized adopted children. *Journal of the American Academy of Child and Adolescent Psychiatry, 27,* 628-631.

Schachter, S., & Singer, J. (1962). Cognitive, social, and physiological determinants of emotional state. *Psychological Review, 69,* 379-399.

Schechter, M., & Bertocci, D. (1990). The meaning of the search. In D.M. Brodzinsky and M.D. Schechter, (Eds.). The psychology of adoption. New York, N.Y.: Oxford University Press, pp 62-91.

Schenck, C., Braver, S. L., Wolchik, S., Saenz, D., Cookston, J., & Fabricius, W. (2000). Relations between Mattering to Step- and Non-Residential Fathers and Adolescent Mental Health. *Fathering, 7*(1), 70-90.

Schneider, D. (1980). American kinship: A cultural account. Second Edition. Chicago: University of Chicago Press.

Shapiro, V., Shapiro J., & Paret, I. (2001). International adoption and the formation of new family attachments. *Smith College Studies in Social Work, 71(3),* 389-418.

Singer, L. M., Brodzinsky, D. M., Steir, M., and Waters, E. (1985). *Child Development, 56,* 1543-1551.

Smith, D. W., & Brodzinsky, D. M. (2002). Coping with birth-parent loss in adopted children. *Journal of Child Psychology and Psychiatry and Allied Disciplines, 43,* 213-223.

Sobol, M. P. (1994, November). The future of adoption in Canada. Keynote address presented at the 2nd annual Gift of Hope Conference, Winnipeg, Manitoba.

Sobol, M. P., & Cardiff, J. (1983). A sociopsychological investigation of adult adoptees' search for birth parents. *Family Relations, 32(4),* 477-483.

Sobol, M. P., & Daly, K. (1994). Canadian adoption statistics: 1981-1990. *Journal of Marriage and the Family, 56,* 493-499.

Sobol, M. P., Daly, K., & Kelloway, K. (2000). Paths to the Facilitation of Open Adoption. *Family Relations, 49*, 419-424.

Sobol, M. P. & Hundlby, J. (November, 1993). Sex, drugs and delinquent behavior of adolescents raised in adopted, step and consanguineous families. Paper presented at the Annual Conference of the National Council on Family Relations, Denver, CO.

Solomon, G. E., Johnson, S. C., Zatichik, D., & Carey, S. (1996). Like father, like son: Young children's understanding of how and why offspring resemble their parents. *Child Development, 67*, 151-171.

Spence, D.P. (1982). Narrative Truth and Historical Truth. New York, N.Y.: W.W Norton and Company.

Stein, L. M., & Hoopes, J. L. (1985). Identity formation in the adopted adolescent. New York: Child Welfare League of America.

Streissguth, A. P., Barr, H. M., Bookstein, F. L., Sampson, P. D., & Olson, H. C. (1999). The long term neurocognitive consequences of prenatal alcohol exposure: A 14-year study. *Psychological Science, 10*, 186-190.

Terrell, J., & Modell, J. (1994). Anthropology and adoption. *American Anthropologist, 96*, 155-161.

Tizard, B. (1977). Adoption: A second chance. New York: The Free Press.

Tizard, B., & Hodges, J. (1978). The effect of early institutional rearing on the development of eight-year-old children. *Journal of Child Psychology and Psychiatry, 19*, 99-118.

Triseliotis, J., & Hill, M. (1990). Contrasting adoption, foster care and residential rearing. In D. Brodzinsky and M. Schechter (Eds.), The psychology of adoption (pp-107-120). New York: Oxford University Press.

Verhulst, F. C., Althaus, M., & Versluis-Den Bieman, H, J. M. (1990). Problem behavior in international adoptees: II. Age at placement. *Journal of the American Academy of Child and Adolescent Psychiatry, 29*, 104-111.

Verhulst, F. C., Althaus, M., & Versluis-Den Bieman, H, J. M. (1992). Damaging backgrounds: Later adjustment of international adoptees. *Journal of the American Academy of Child and Adolescent Psychiatry, 31*, 518-524.

Verrier, N. (1987). The primal wound: A preliminary investigation into the effects of separation from the birth mother on adopted children. *Pre- and Peri-Natal Psychology, 2*, 75-86.

Verrier, N. (1993). The primal wound: Understanding the adopted child. Baltimore: Gateway Press.

Warren, S. B. (1992). Lower threshold for referral for psychiatric treatment for adopted adolescents. *Journal of the American Academy of Child and Adolescent Psychiatry, 31*, 518-524.

Watkins, M., & Fisher, S. (1993). Talking with young children about adoption. New Haven, CT: Yale University Press.

Weiss, A. (1985). Symptomatology of adopted and nonadopted adolescents in a psychiatric hospital. *Adolescence, 20*, 763-774.

Wilson, T. D. (2002). Strangers to ourselves: Discovering the adaptive unconscious. Cambridge, MA: Belknap Press.

Winkler, R., & van Keppel, M. (1984). Relinquishing mothers in adoption: Their long-term adjustment. Melbourne, AU: Institute of Family Studies.

Michael Grand received his PhD in Clinical Psychology from the State University of New York at Stony Brook. He is a Professor in the Child Clinical Psychology Graduate Program at the University of Guelph in Guelph, Ontario, Canada. He co-directed the National Adoption Study of Canada and has published extensively on search and reunion, adoptive identity, sense of family, demographics of adoption, paths to openness and factors affecting outcome in adoption. He is the recipient of the David Kirk Award for outstanding contributions to research in adoption. He has served as a board member of the Adoption Council of Canada and the Adoption Council of Ontario. As a founding member of the coordinating committee of the Coalition for Open Adoption Records, he continues to work for access to identifying information for all. Dr Grand has a private therapy practice for members of the adoption constellation.